Other People's Money

Theoretical Lenses on Public Policy

Series Editor, Paul A. Sabatier

Other People's Money

Policy Change, Congress, and Bank Regulation

Jeffrey Worsham

West Virginia University

■ WestviewPress
A Division of HarperCollins*Publishers*

To Debby Kayoko

Theoretical Lenses on Public Policy

Copyright © 1997 by Westview Press, A Division of HarperCollins Publishers, Inc.

Published in 1997 in the United States of America by Westview Press, 5500 Central Avenue, Boulder,
Colorado 80301-2877, and in the United Kingdom by Westview Press, 12 Hid's Copse Road, Cumnor
Hill, Oxford OX2 9JJ

Library of Congress Cataloging-in-Publication Data

Worsham, Jeffrey.
   Other people's money : policy change, Congress, and bank
regulation / Jeffrey Worsham.
       p.   cm.—(Theoretical lenses on public policy)
   Includes bibliographical references and index.
   ISBN 0-8133-9953-X (hardcover).—ISBN 0-8133-9952-1 (paperback)
   1. Banks and banking—United States—State supervision.   2. Banks
and banking—Government policy—United States.   3. Pressure groups—
United States.   I. Title.   II. Series.
KF974.W67   1997
346.73'082—dc21   97-6426
                                                                              CIP

The paper used in this publication meets the requirements of the American National Standard for
Permanence of Paper for Printed Library Materials Z39.48-1984.

10   9   8   7   6   5   4   3   2   1

Contents

Tables and Figures

Acronyms

ABA	American Bankers Association
ATM	automatic teller machine
CUNA	Credit Union National Association
DIDC	Depository Institutions Deregulation Committee
DIDMCA	Depository Institutions Deregulation and Monetary Control Act
EFT	electronic fund transfer
FDIC	Federal Deposit Insurance Corporation
FHLBB	Federal Home Loan Bank Board
Fed	Federal Reserve Board
FINE	Financial Institutions and the Nation's Economy
FSLIC	Federal Savings and Loan Insurance Corporation
IBAA	Independent Bankers Association of America
MMDA	money market demand account
MMF	money market fund
NCC	National Credit Corporation
NCUA	National Credit Union Administration
NLISA	National League of Insured Savings Associations
NMC	National Monetary Commission
NOW	negotiable order of withdrawal
NSLL	National Savings and Loan League
NYCHC	New York Clearing House Committee
OCC	Office of the Comptroller of the Currency
OMC	Open Market Committee
OTS	Office of Thrift Supervision
RFC	Reconstruction Finance Corporation
RTC	Resolution Trust Corporation
SEC	Securities and Exchange Commission
USLSA	United States League of Savings Associations
USSLA	United States Savings and Loan Association

Acknowledgments

This book offers an explanation of policymaking that builds on the work of a variety of scholars. Ken Meier, Cathy Johnson, Chuck Jones, and Graham Wilson were mentors at the University of Wisconsin, where I obtained my Ph.D. It was their collective humor, patience, and insight that got the ball rolling in my work on subsystems. My colleagues in the Department of Political Science at West Virginia University, especially Kevin Leyden and John Kilwin as well as numerous panel chairs and discussants (you know who you are) at several professional conferences provided several occasions—formal and informal—for me to bounce ideas off them, rattle on about financial regulation, and generally bore them with the world of subsystems. For this they deserve thanks. The government-documents librarians at West Virginia University—Keven Fredette, Christine Chang, and Marian Armour-Gemman—guided me through the morass that makes up any library's government-documents collection. Paul Sabatier as series editor and informal copy editor, Diane Hess as official copy editor, Melanie Stafford as associate project editor, Leo Wiegman as editor and lunch provider, and an anonymous reviewer provided valuable input. Finally, my wife contributed to this project in so many ways that it is as much her book as mine. Her patience in listening to me work my way through the project "one more time" during our walks to work, over dinner, while working out or watching a movie—you get the picture—earns her not only thanks but a promise not to discuss the second book unless she brings it up first.

Jeffrey Worsham

Doing the Subsystem Two-Step

In sum, the American political system is a mosaic
of continually reshaping systems of limited participation.
(Baumgartner and Jones 1993, 6)

Why study subsystems? Because that is where the action is. This simple truth is too often overlooked. Subsystems developed as a solution to the problem of making policy in the rough and tumble world of the American polity. Their growth parallels the development of the congressional committee system and the administrative state. Indeed, they are intimately linked to both. Through a combination of historical case studies of key periods of institutional and ideational change, and more systematic empirical documentation of interest group politics, this study traces not only the evolution of the financial subsystem but offers an explanation for its longevity.

SUBSYSTEM MODELS OF POLICYMAKING

Questions of influence are at the heart of political science. Harold Lasswell's (1958) question of "who gets what, when, how" still guides most studies of American politics. Lasswell answered his own question by suggesting that well-organized interests, which he deemed elites, commanded the lion's share of resources, public and private. The key to securing a share of public policy, then, was organization (Lasswell 1958, 172–173). The notion that organization into interest groups was fundamental to a fair distribution of resources reflected the dominant motif of American political science in the 1950s—pluralism.[1]

Pluralist political theory is as old as the American republic. James Madison, writing as Publius, discussed the mischief and mechanics of factions, by which he meant interest groups and parties, in *Federalist 10*. Mark Petracca (1992, 3) suggests Thomas Paine was among the first to propose that interest groups or factions undermined the public good by pursuing their own self-interest. What distinguished Madison from Paine was Madison's ability to reconcile the existence of interest groups with a polity that still managed to pursue the public interest, at least most of the time. Madison suggested that the federal design of government allowed the system to harness interest group energies and channel them in such a way so as to produce policy that served the public interest.

Nearly 200 years later, Truman (1951), Latham (1952), and Dahl (1961) reinvigorated the pluralist model of politics with a renewed focus on the role of interest groups in the policy process. Their answer to Lasswell's question was a good deal more optimistic than either Paine's or Lasswell's. They suggested that political power was scattered among a wide and varied set of public and private interests throughout the U.S. polity. In keeping with Madison, they emphasized that although power and resources might be unevenly distributed in the polity as a whole, "those inequalities were dispersed and noncumulative" (Petracca 1992, 5). In this view, the fragmented nature of political institutions both prevented the concentration of public and private power and also provided multiple access points for a wide variety of interests to present their demands. In this fashion democracy was served, indeed guaranteed, by the actions of competing interest groups. Pluralists were rather sanguine with regard to the role of interest groups because they assumed all citizens either belonged to such organizations or could join or form interest groups if the need arose. Robert Dahl (1961) argued it was the balance between active and latent groups that produced a democratic equilibrium. The pluralists suggested that competition among interest groups, actual and potential, determined who got what, when, and how, but some observers of public policy were not so sure.

Picking up on Lasswell's observations concerning the role of elites in garnering the largest piece of the policy pie, subsystem theorists argued that the highly disaggregated governmental structure of the American polity provides plenty of opportunity for well-organized interest groups to carve out a niche for themselves. Once they gain a toehold, interest groups create an alliance with legislative and bureaucratic specialists that takes the form of a policy monopoly the central purpose of which is to avoid interest group competition (Baumgartner and Jones 1993; Thurber 1991). The end result, as described by Woodrow Wilson (1885, 76) over 100 years ago, is that "power is nowhere concentrated; it is rather deliberately and of set policy scattered amongst many small chiefs." Subsystems theory, then, suggests that policymaking functions of government have been assumed by cabals of special interest groups. The strongest enunciation of this thesis is by Theodore Lowi (1969), who argues that the idealized "government by the people, for the people" has become government by select interest groups for select interest groups.

Still, not all observers agree. Whereas there is a consensus that influence is increasingly concentrated in, and exercised by, subsystems, there is some disagreement over the identity of the beneficiaries of subsystem politics. The confusion over who, exactly, benefits from subsystem arrangements is a result of the variety of studies that have used the subsystem framework in slightly different ways. That is, although the subsystem model is the lingua franca of those studying public policy, there are several distinct dialects spoken by adherents. Whirlpools, iron triangles, capture, issue networks, sloppy large hexagons, presence politics, and advocacy coalitions have all been offered as subsystem-based frameworks of analysis. From Hugh Heclo's (1978) observation that the iron triangle concept was incomplete to more recent studies that trace the weakening or end of subsystems altogether (Bosso 1987; Balogh 1991), there is growing disagreement over the identity of beneficiaries of subsystem arrangements, the goods provided by such arrangements, and the staying power of subsystems. Focusing on the increasing diversity and number of interest groups involved in policymaking, some observers argue subsystems have evolved from fairly closed affairs to something akin to the free-for-all of classic interest group politics (Heclo 1978; Jones 1984; Gais, Peterson, and Walker 1984; Baumgartner and Jones 1993).

If we focus on the identity of participants, the subsystem literature can be arranged into several camps. Two major camps have developed around particular variants of subsystem arrangements—iron triangles and issue networks—but the wide variety of subsystem flora are best understood through the integration of the work of Paul Sabatier and Hank Jenkins-Smith (1993) with that of James Thurber (1991). Utilizing Sabatier and Jenkins-Smith's notion of advocacy coalitions and Thurber's schema of subsystem political variation, one can distinguish three variations of subsystem politics—dominant coalitions, transitory coalitions, and competing coalitions. The following brief review of each variant of subsystem politics is offered to provide a better feel for the variety of subsystem players, political styles, and policy outcomes possible under the subsystem rubric.

Dominant Coalitions

Dominant-coalition politics are reminiscent of the classic iron triangle.[2] At one time the terms iron triangle and subsystem were used interchangeably in political science. The model was developed by students of public policy who, in their study of a particular program or policy area, documented the existence of policy-specific "alliances cutting across the two branches of government and including key operatives from outside" the government (Cater 1964, 17). Because of their seemingly static membership—members of select congressional committees, agency personnel, and interest groups affected by the policy in question—these arrangements were christened "iron triangles."

Iron triangle theorists model a world in which budget-maximizing bureaucrats and reelection-seeking legislators do what self-seeking interest groups demand. The result is policy that favors select interests over the "public interest," expands the budget and responsibilities of agency personnel, and ensures the reelection of legislators on oversight committees. Quite simply, policy produced by dominant coalitions "serves the private interests of politically effective groups" (Posner 1974, 343). Dominant coalitions specialize in the development and delivery of distributive policy (Thurber 1991, 327–329), that is, policy that benefits select interests and is paid for, unknowingly, by the public. In the case of economic regulation this usually means the majority of regulation "is acquired by the industry and is designed and operated primarily for its benefit" (Stigler 1971, 3).

Although the dominant-coalition model is grounded in group theory, competition among interests in a dominant-coalition setting is nonexistent or relatively unimportant. Indeed, the rationale underlying the formation of a subsystem is that it allows subsystem members to shun competition for control and predictability. Subsystem participants establish rule structures, or institutions, that defuse potential conflict through a "just" distribution of valued resources. Congressional committees serve this purpose through the establishment of a policy monopoly (Baumgartner and Jones 1993).

Congress is the obvious institutional variable that explains the staying power of subsystem arrangements. A variety of studies demonstrates how legislative careerism and policy complexity contribute to the growth of subsystem policymaking. Most agree that the organizational features of Congress, "in particular, its accessibility to outside influences, its weak central leadership, its decentralization, its bargaining ethos, and its norms of specialization and reciprocity," form an ideal setting for subsystem policymaking (Davidson 1977, 30).[3] All these factors come together and are embodied in the committee system. Congressional committees, and subcommittees in particular, are decisionmaking systems that are "heavily predisposed toward the very interests under their purview" (Davidson 1977, 33). Legislators choose committee assignments based upon their ability to serve constituents. The committee system, and the proliferation of subcommittees, produce congressional fragmentation, which "encourages and reinforces the development of tightly knit [subsystem] relationships between interest groups and federal agencies" (Aberbach and Rockman 1978, 818; Thurber 1991; Baumgartner and Jones 1993).

Theoretically, macrolevel government institutions—Congress, the White House, the courts—serve as the ultimate parameters in which subsystems are nested. The dominant-coalition approach, however, assumes subsystem policy decisions are routinely approved by actors in the larger political system. Thus dominant coalitions are highly autonomous in the pursuit of member goals through legislation. The ability of dominant coalitions to maintain "closure upon decisions affecting them" depends on two factors—the degree of competition among component groups in the subsystem and the degree of public visibility associated with any given issue (Davidson 1977, 35; Hamm 1983; Gormley 1986; Baumgartner and Jones 1993). Dominant coalitions thrive under conditions of little competition and low issue salience.

When subsystem players are unable to reach a compromise (that is, competition increases) or the issue at hand is one that draws the attention of outsiders, policy formation is less likely to be as restricted as depicted by the dominant-coalition scenario (Meier 1985, 11). Noting the increasing frequency of just this situation in the 1970s, several observers documented a new variant of subsystem politics (Heclo 1978; Ripley and Franklin 1987; Bosso 1987).

Transitory Coalitions

Although the traditional notion of a subsystem "presumes small circles of participants who have succeeded in becoming largely autonomous," subsystems characterized by transitory coalitions contain "a large number of participants with quite variable degrees of mutual commitment or of dependence on others in their environment" (Heclo 1978, 102). Rather than containing a relatively small and stable set of participants, as is the dominant-coalition norm, transitory coalitions represent the merry-go-round of subsystems. Select players move in and out of the system in an apparently random manner. "Rather than groups united in dominance over a program, no one, as far as one can tell, is in control of the policies and issues" (Heclo 1978, 102). Notable among new participants are organized groups of outsiders, often allied with representatives of the president, legislators who are not members of the oversight committee, or policy intellectuals. Presidents and stray legislators are often acting as agenda setters at the behest of outsiders. Policy intellectuals serve as "idea entrepreneurs," providing new paradigms for understanding policy options.

The participation of these newcomers means that the material outcome of policy produced in a transitory-coalition setting is potentially more varied than is the case with dominant coalitions. Transitory subsystems tend to produce a mix of redistributive policy—with redistribution often occurring among subsystem-based factions—and regulatory policy, in which the actions of a particular class of private actors are subject to increased government scrutiny (Thurber 1991, 330).

Despite the new cast of players and shift in policy, transitory coalitions are rarely as chaotic as Heclo suggests. This is because outsiders and their institutional allies are but temporary sojourners on the subsystem scene. Presidents suffer from resource constraints, a wider variety of programmatic responsibilities, and a deficiency in knowledge, none of which allow them the constant vigilance practiced by committee members, agency personnel, and select private interests. Similarly, academics and their ideas usually enjoy a brief flurry of attention only to fade into policy oblivion once their "fifteen minutes of fame" are up. Finally, if a legislator wishes to exercise long-term influence in a policy realm, she must find a way to get on the committee charged with oversight responsibility.

Transitory coalitions, then, involve politics in which participation has been expanded as a result of shared interest, knowledge, and expertise in a particular policy area. Still, the list of players is limited and their involvement is fleeting. Newcomers often modify items on the subsystem agenda through a reallocation of resources among subsystem players and increased regulation of select activity but rarely enjoy the staying power necessary to shape policy in a lasting way. Rather, when challengers appear on the subsystem scene and stick around, one has yet another variant of subsystem politics—competitive coalitions.

Competitive Coalitions

Competitive coalitions can be distinguished from dominant coalitions by the increasing diversity of interests involved in subsystem deal making. Unlike the case of transitory coalitions, outsiders are well organized, are motivated by a mix of material self-interest and policy expertise, and are long-term players.[4] Outsiders are often members of another subsystem responding to perceived threats to the autonomy of their home base (Ripley and Franklin 1987). In some cases they are simply newcomers to the interest group setting, looking for a subsystem niche of their own (Browne 1988). They may even be homegrown challengers who previously enjoyed minority-coalition status in the subsystem (Sabatier and Jenkins-Smith 1993). Competitive coalitions are reminiscent of what Christopher Bosso (1987, 246) refers to as "presence politics." In presence politics, interests fight to establish and maintain their presence in a particular subsystem. Much of the struggle involves establishing the legitimacy of their previously unrecognized claim(s) to a piece of the policy pie. Bosso argued this is primarily an intellectual enterprise involving competition among experts over hard-to-understand points of fact, but it ultimately boils down to a struggle over both policy outputs (material interests) and underlying ideas.

Unlike transitory coalitions, competitive coalitions involve a quite regular collection of interests. Despite this regularity, outsiders do not seek compromise solutions based on shared interest, as do their dominant-coalition cousins. Rather, they seek to alter the distribution of scarce resources, often through alteration of the rules that serve as the institutional basis of the subsystem. Thus, the committee system in competitive coalitions is characterized by turf wars among standing committees, joint and split referral of legislation, an increasing loss of civility in the chamber, and instability of committee-authored arrangements. Quite simply, norms of deference and logrolling are under increasing scrutiny and challenge. Outsiders challenge the mutual noninterference pact that serves as the guiding principle of the committee system in dominant coalitions. Conflict between insiders (subsystem players) and outsiders (challengers) results in an increasing number of attempts to alter the venue of decisionmaking—to the outsiders home turf (committee), a neutral committee, or the floor of the chamber itself (see Jones, Baumgartner, and Talbert 1993, for an extended discussion of venue switching).

Competitors seek to alter the decisionmaking venue because they want to replace distributive or mildly redistributive policy with more radically redistributive (from the vantage of subsystem players) policy. They often seek to force insiders to pay the hidden costs of policy, in effect redistributing costs back to insiders. They may also seek to prevent subsystem players from advancing into new policy territory—either through enforcement of existing regulatory prohibitions or by rewriting regulation to create such prohibitions. Competitive coalitions, then, are subsystems under prolonged stress.

Making Sense of the Subsystem Morass

The preceding review of the subsystem literature suggests that the answer to Lasswell's query concerning who gets what depends on the particular variant of subsystem politics operating at a given point in time. Subsystem politics are shaped both by large-scale social, economic, and political change and by the strategic interaction of individuals within a particular policy community or subsystem (Heclo 1974 and 1978; Sabatier and Jenkins-Smith 1993). Each variant of subsystem politics involves a different mix of external (environmental) and internal (subsystem) variables, which in turn produce different types of policy.

Dominant coalitions are subsystems in which the policy minuet is danced to a tune composed almost exclusively by subsystem participants. That is, subsystem insiders are highly autonomous in deciding what to do and how to do it. In transitory coalitions, subsystem players dance to a score that is jointly composed by insiders and outsiders, often in response to events in the larger environment. The involvement of the president, academics, or stray legislators forces subsystem insiders to alter policy in an attempt to head off deeper involvement by outsiders. Under competitive coalitions, insiders are unable to insulate themselves, and the policy process, from outsider demands and environmental forces. Subsystem insiders, buffeted by the demands of outsiders as well as events unfolding in the larger environment must compromise on policy solutions or risk the complete loss of control of the process.

Subsystem autonomy in deciding the shape of policy, then, is not uniform and constant through time. Rather, autonomy is affected by the ability of key players to reach mutually agreeable bargains and by external (to the subsystem) events. What explains the expansion (and contraction) of interests involved in subsystem policymaking? The preceding literature review hinted at several possibilities that the following section explores in greater detail.

EXPLAINING SUBSYSTEM VARIATION OVER TIME

Frank Baumgartner and Bryan Jones (1993, 7) suggest that "policy monopolies [subsystems] have two important characteristics. First, a definable institutional structure is responsible for policymaking, and that structure limits access to the policy process. Second, a powerful supporting idea is associated with the institution." Explaining subsystem change, then, involves identifying challenges to the institutional structure(s) and change in the underlying idea(s) associated with each variant of subsystem politics.

The preceding review of subsystem models suggests that the institutional structure common to all subsystems is the congressional committee system. The ability of committees to protect their turf—indeed, often the mere challenge to committee turf—is what distinguishes one subsystem variant from another. Challenges to subsystem arrangements, then, come in two basic forms—environmental change and challenges from actors outside the subsystem. The ability of committees to preserve their autonomy is dependent on a variety of factors. Among the variables that weaken committee autonomy and encourage the expansion of participation in the policy process are institutional conflict, party politics, media attention, and economic dislocation. All these may contribute to changes in prevailing ideas. Indeed, they are intimately linked.

The following discussion focuses on the activities of national institutions, interest groups, and events. This is probably too narrow an emphasis given that Keith Hamm has identified the subsystem phenomenon as operating at the state level. Given my focus on federal regulatory policy and in the interest of keeping the reader's attention, I restrict the discussion to national-level variables. Those interested in state-level subsystems can substitute "executive" for "president," "legislature" for "Congress," and with some other minor modifications test the framework at the state level.

Institutional Conflict

The U.S. system of "separate institutions sharing powers" is one in which conflict is expected. Such conflict also explains why the subsystem solution leads to such a fragile equilibrium. Sooner or later subsystem arrangements run afoul of the natural antagonism programmed into our system of government. Institutional conflict can occur in a variety of dimensions. The most obvious involves the major elected institutions of government—the executive and legislature—as antagonists. In addition, Congress itself presents a series of institutional variables that shape and challenge subsystem arrangements.

The president. The most high-profile attempt to alter subsystem arrangements involves presidential intrusions into subsystem affairs. Subsystems are creatures of domestic politics and policy. They exist as mechanisms for meeting demands of powerful interests for a share of the policy pie. The bulk of presidential attention is focused on foreign policy concerns, but every president makes an occasional foray into the congressional preserve of domestic politics. Indeed, some occupants of the Oval Office stand out for their attempt to reorient major domestic policies and programs. Theodore Roosevelt as "trust buster," Franklin Roosevelt's New Deal, Lyndon Johnson's Great Society, Richard Nixon's administrative presidency strategy, and Ronald Reagan's New Federalism are all examples of presidential activism on the domestic front. When a president dabbles in domestic policy, it is usually an attempt to alter the benefit calculus established by subsystem players.

In addition to the more visible domestic initiatives, most presidents experiment with more generic administrative reforms. These attempts to "rationalize" the bureaucratic machinery are often portrayed as efforts to enhance managerial powers of the executive in purely efficiency terms (Light 1995; Ingraham and Rosenbloom 1992). Still, attempts to alter organizational features of specific departments, agencies, or bureaus cannot help but have an impact on subsystem arrangements. As such, presidential attempts to reorganize, streamline, or otherwise alter existing organizational features of the bureaucracy are usually viewed with suspicion by subsystem players.

Presidential attempts to alter subsystem arrangements are usually associated with the enthusiasm of the newcomer. That is, they are something most new occupants of the office experiment with in the first year or so in office. As the prospects for success dim, presidential resources dwindle, appointees settle in, or legislation is passed, most chief executives lose interest in the nitty-gritty of subsystem politics. Presidents may prove quite successful in gaining access to the subsystem agenda but prove less able to see issues through to the end of the process (Schroedel 1994). Thus, although an important institutional dynamic, the executive as a force for change is often overshadowed by congressionally based forces.

Congress. Given its role in subsystem arrangements, it is no surprise that Congress provides some of the more important institutional dynamics affecting subsystem autonomy. Remember, subsystems are congressional creatures. They are congressionally authored solutions to the problems of increasing policy complexity and programmatic responsibility. Like their institutional incarnation, the committee system, subsystems allow members to parcel out policy responsibility and partition interest group demands in a fashion that allows the chamber to function in a relatively efficient and responsive manner. Thus, subsystems depend on the acquiescence of the chamber as a whole to committee prerogatives for their survival. When subsystem arrangements fail to function as envisioned, they come under increasing scrutiny and challenge from members in the chamber at large. Such challenge may take the form of alterations in the rules governing the chamber, the referral of legislation, committee memberships, and the structure of the committee system itself.

An important challenge to subsystem institutional autonomy takes the form of increased scrutiny of committee activity. One indicator of such scrutiny involves the introduction of legislation dealing with subsystem policy responsibilities. Bill introduction by noncommittee members increases as nonexpert legislators try their hand at agenda setting and problem solving. Such an increase is often the first indicator of dissatisfaction with subsystem-authored arrangements. Similarly, the actions of policy committees may be subject to challenge from rival committees or the leadership of the chamber. An increase in multiple referrals or joint referrals or a complete change of venue are all indications that subsystems are losing their policy monopoly (Baumgartner and Jones 1993). When bills are sent to other committees, agenda control is in serious doubt.

Similarly, a change in committee membership or chair may affect the universe of interests involved in the policy process. The impact of such change is often mediated by whether it involves a change in party control of the chamber as well as the nature of policy dealt with by the committee. Using Richard Fenno's (1973) classification of committee types, one can argue that changes in party control of constituent service committees will produce less disruption than similar changes in policy committees. This is because policy committees are often the site of pitched battles between Republican and Democratic ideologues, whereas constituent service committees work in a bipartisan fashion. So, for example, a switch in party control should have less effect on the Agriculture Committee and its relationship with important clientele than it would have on Education and Labor.

Another congressional dynamic involves the relationship between chambers. Quite simply, although both the House and Senate are representative bodies, there is a built-in rivalry between the two that often affects subsystem autonomy (Baker 1989; Longley and Oleszek 1989). In addition, the Senate and House are known to operate in quite different fashions. Committee autonomy and turf are more jealously guarded in the House than in the Senate. One might suggest, then, that subsystem bonds are stronger in the House than the Senate. Similarly, each chamber also views presidential intrusions in a different light, a phenomenon compounded by the interaction of party as a variable. The possibility of split party control—with one chamber controlled by the GOP and the other in the hands of the Democrats—adds an additional wrinkle to this intrainstitutional dynamic.

Party Politics

The preceding discussion of institutional factors touches on an important variable impacting subsystem autonomy—party politics. Several observers of the subsystem phenomenon note that when a subsystem's policy responsibilities become the subject of party politics, subsystem autonomy suffers (Davidson 1977; Meier 1985; Baumgartner and Jones 1993; Sabatier and Jenkins-Smith 1993). The actual impact of party-related challenges depends on the locus of change.

Change in party control of the White House, although important, may have a less direct effect on subsystem autonomy than change in party control of one or both chambers of Congress. This is because institutional factors alone explain a good deal of presidential interest in subsystem affairs. Presidents can be expected to attempt to dabble in subsystem business regardless of their party affiliation. The attempt may intensify when the White House is subject to a shift in party control, but the nature of the attempt is still primarily interinstitutional and subject to the declining-resources scenario painted by Paul Light (1982).

Congressionally centered change, in contrast, produces a ripple effect—beginning with the leadership of the chamber, proceeding down through the chairs of committees and subcommittees and the membership on committees, and ending with a new dynamic on the floor itself. Party change that affects the membership of Congress, the "keystone" of subsystem arrangements, can be expected to have a more direct effect on subsystems, an effect that is, as mentioned previously, mediated by the type of committee serving as the subsystem bedrock. Constituent committees that pursue pork for subsystem members in a bipartisan fashion are not as vulnerable as their more ideologically divided counterparts. Still, a change in the dominant party in either chamber, especially if accompanied by a change in party control of the executive, can be expected to have an important impact on subsystem arrangements (Sabatier and Jenkins-Smith 1993, 22).

Media Attention

Issue salience is the bane of subsystems. The more people know *of* a particular program and the more they know *about* it, the harder it is to restrict participation in the program or policy area. William Gormley (1986) suggests that increased salience (how many people know of a program) and decreased complexity (what they know about it) is a fatal combination for subsystems. Increased salience attracts a whole host of outsiders intent on getting in on a piece of the subsystem action. Low technical complexity allows outsiders to get more easily involved in subsystem policymaking because knowledge, or more accurately a lack of knowledge, does not serve as a barrier keeping out all but the experts. The degree of complexity associated with banking policy remains consistently high over time, but salience varies. Frank R. Baumgartner and Bryan D. Jones (1993, 103) suggest that a "major source of instability in American politics is the shifting attention of the media." No one knows this better than subsystem players. Salience-raising media attention is to be avoided at all costs. In the eyes of subsystem regulars, no news is good news because getting an item on the public (media) agenda is often the first step in an outsider's attempt to influence subsystem policy. Quite simply, as salience increases, more outsiders are attracted to subsystem affairs. Increased media attention is associated with presidential attempts at agenda setting, open and heated "expert" debate over the best course of policy, and outright attempts to move in on subsystem turf by outsiders; such activities are typical of transitory and competitive coalitions.

Economic Dislocation

The iron triangle variation of subsystem theory argues that subsystems develop as a means of distributing the spoils of the policy process. That is, they are primarily vehicles for the transmission of economic benefits to well-organized private interests while spreading the (hidden) costs among outsiders. It is when the hidden costs become obvious, or when insider benefits dry up, that dominant coalitions are subject to challenge.

Economic dislocation places stress on both subsystem insiders and outsiders. Recession, depression, inflation, rising unemployment, a slowdown in economic growth, and budget deficits all make the costs of subsystem-brokered policy more obvious. Zero-sum politics becomes the norm. Winners and losers are brought face to face by the shrinking economic pie. A key mechanism of subsystem strength, the ability to hide and spread the costs of subsystem goodies, no longer functions smoothly. Subsystem bargains prove impossible to honor, causing defection and dissension within the subsystem. Increasingly, subsystem players pursue policy goals that can be realized only at the expense of other subsystem actors.

Latent tension within a subsystem is often exacerbated by economic events; when previously unnoticed costs become obvious to those paying them, subsystem policies are subject to increasing challenge and attempts at outsider participation in decisionmaking. Outsiders challenge not only the distribution of benefits and costs but the underlying rationale of many subsystem programs. This outsider challenge to subsystem beliefs introduces yet another important vehicle of change—ideas.

Ideas

Shared material interests, and the distribution of benefits vis-à-vis public policy, form bonds of mutual interest among subsystem players, but ideas are the glue that holds subsystems together. Gary Mucciaroni (1990, 258) writes, "Policies are not simply reflections of political and institutional power. They are intellectual creations as well." Although the focus of a pure interest group approach is on the material self-interest of actors and how this shapes group dynamics—the stuff of iron triangle approaches in subsystems theory—policy is not always the result of folks simply pursuing material interests. Rather, policy involves a mix of goals—ranging from the simple pursuit of base material interests to attempts to realize some political or social ideal via public policy.

The advocacy-coalition framework of Paul Sabatier and Hank Jenkins-Smith (1993, 16) captures this ideational mix through an examination of belief systems. The argument in brief is that "public policies (or programs) can be conceptualized in the same manner as belief systems, that is, as sets of value priorities and causal assumptions about how to realize them." Sabatier and Jenkins-Smith offer a three-tiered model of belief systems that aids in the identification of coalitions active in any particular subsystem and also goes a long way in explaining policy change over time. I use a variation of their model that emphasizes two elements of belief systems—policy core beliefs and programmatic components.[5] I also suggest that belief systems serve as an institutional bulwark of a subsystem. That is, they form a subsystem ideology that most members subscribe to consciously and unconsciously. As such, they are part of a larger gestalt, or regime, of ideas and institutions that serve to guide policymaking in a particular political system (see Eisner 1993).

Policy core beliefs, consisting of fundamental policy positions, are often unique to particular subsystems and serve to distinguish members of one system from those of another. Similarly to Sabatier and Jenkins-Smith (1993, 219–221), I argue that the policy core consists of two components: The first contains fundamental normative precepts; the second consists of ideas with a substantial empirical component or basis. The notion of normative and empirical components is of course a heuristic. In reality, it is hard to separate the two or identify a purely normative or empirical belief. Still, the notion is useful in identifying components of beliefs that unite coalitions and serve as the basis of much of public policy.

So, for example, in the case of financial regulation, a key normative element of the policy core since the 1930s is the belief that markets are destructive. This idea has an empirical basis in the speculation and risk taking with "other peoples money" that had disastrous results in the late nineteenth century and culminated in the Great Depression; it assumed a near-sacred quality through the 1970s. Thus the notion that markets are destructive, at least in the realm of banking, became an unquestioned truism of the financial subsystem. Closely related to this normative policy belief is the empirical idea that regulation should promote controlled competition in the provision of financial services. That is, whereas uncontrolled competition might be destructive, channeled competition promotes the benefits of the market without the costs. The trick becomes how to translate beliefs into working policy; enter programmatic beliefs.

In Sabatier and Jenkins-Smith's model, secondary aspects "comprising a multitude of instrumental decisions and information searches necessary to implement the policy core in the specific policy area" provide another essential element of belief systems (Sabatier and Jenkins-Smith 1993, 30). I argue that these beliefs are manifested as actual programs and as such may divide subsystem members into distinct coalitions—depending on perceived benefits and costs associated with a particular program. Programmatic beliefs, then, are the physical manifestation of policy core beliefs. They are attempts to realize more abstract core beliefs by translating policy goals into actual programs—regulation, distributive policy, and the like.

In the case of financial regulation, subsystem actors have experimented with a variety of programs in an attempt to realize policy goals. New Deal regulation that separated financial intermediaries according to function—commercial banks dealt primarily with short-term business loans, savings and loans with longer-term home loans, credit unions with short-term borrowing, and so on—is a prime example of a key programmatic element of the financial-subsystem belief system. Although this separation-by-function programmatic element provided for competition, such competition was to occur between intermediaries of the same type and under conditions closely monitored by regulatory authorities.

Under dominant coalitions it appears that the only beliefs of importance are the programmatic elements of the belief system. This is because policy core beliefs are rarely examined, let alone called into question (Sabatier and Jenkins-Smith 1993, 226; Stewart 1991). Rather, most of "the action" involves debate over the distribution of resources. This is not meant to suggest that policy core beliefs are unimportant, simply that they are so ingrained that no one challenges them. When policy core beliefs do come under fire, it is often because programmatic incarnations can no longer deliver benefits.

In the case of transitory coalitions, players question the distribution of resources resulting from programmatic elements of the belief system. The challenge is often offered as a variation on beliefs making up the policy core, not so much calling the policy core beliefs themselves into question but the manner in which they are realized via specific programs. The challenge, then, is a question of interpretation based on shared knowledge or expertise that primarily affects programmatic aspects. Economists, for example, have been known to argue that the controlled competition promoted by separation-by-function principles hurts more consumers than it helps. Although not calling for the abandonment of financial regulation, they suggest that competition between different types of financial intermediaries—banks and savings and loans, for example—would better serve consumers. They call for widening the scope of competition while still maintaining regulatory controls.

Competitive coalitions challenge policy core beliefs. They too want to alter programs, but they base their challenge on a different set of policy core beliefs. These beliefs often serve as the basis of another subsystem and are incompatible with programs and beliefs of the subsystem under challenge. So, for example, in the 1970s a variety of business interests—securities firms, insurance interests, and credit card companies—challenged the policy core belief that banking was different from other forms of commerce. These "nonbank banks" experimented with a variety of financial instruments they claimed did not come under financial regulatory authority but rather were simply extensions of their own business activities.

Challenges to policy core elements of the dominant belief system may cause subsystem members themselves to question, and attempt to alter, subsystem arrangements. The mildest reaction is one that produces an incremental change in programmatic aspects. A more dramatic reaction is one in which subsystem members splinter into rival coalitions. In such instances the minority coalition(s) may be tempted to seek executive-branch allies, as is the case under transitory coalitions; or they may seek to join forces with a coalition in another subsystem or widen the scope of the conflict by recruiting outsiders, as is the case under competitive coalitions. In any case, a focus on beliefs is essential to understanding the dynamic nature of subsystem politics.

The focus on ideas suggests that politics do not simply vary as a direct result of some change in the larger environment. Rather, change in the larger environment—be it institutional, media, economic, or party—is interpreted by human actors who may then alter the way in which they look at the world; their interpretations may then result in a reaffirmation of existing subsystem arrangements or a challenge to the status quo (Brown and Stewart 1993). The mechanism for transmitting stimuli from the larger environment to subsystem players, and vice versa, is usually referred to as "feedback."

Feedback

The "feedback" loop is a staple of all systems models. Yet it all too often goes undefined—no minor oversight, since it is the causal element in systems models. Feedback serves as the transmission belt between subsystem outputs, outcomes, ideas, and politics. As such, it takes the form of information that promotes "policy learning." Such learning may result in alterations in the dominant belief system, or it may reaffirm existing beliefs and subsystem arrangements.

Feedback often takes the form of policy analysis that highlights shortcomings in subsystem-authored solutions to societal problems, necessitating increased scrutiny of subsystem business by the president, Congress, or the courts (Bosso 1987). Or it may involve increased public (media) attention, raising the salience of the policy area or a particular program (Baumgartner and Jones 1993). Christopher Bosso (1987, 237–238) argues that increased awareness leads to more "policy claimants" and greater difficulty in effecting closure on any given issue. Indeed, when previously low-profile issues become the subject of heightened scrutiny, there is a real possibility that subsystems will be "broken up by the intrusion of powerful groups from other areas of the economy" (Baumgartner and Jones 1993, 9).

Still, not all feedback is negative; nor is it high profile. Feedback may appear as evidence in support of policy beliefs or "proof" that the distribution of benefits serves the nation and, not coincidentally, subsystem members. Positive feedback strengthens girding ideas, reinforcing the tendency to defer to subsystem expertise in dealing with particular issues.

The discussion of subsystem dynamics has focused exclusively on the expansion of interests involved in subsystem policymaking. Needless to say, contraction of the cast of subsystem players is another possibility. Contraction occurs as a result of many of the variables discussed earlier—the economy works its way out of a slump, crises pass, new disasters affecting other subsystems worm their way onto the public agenda, battling coalitions reach a mutually satisfactory legislative solution, a president moves on to new areas of interest, or there is a change in administration. The result is that subsystem politics move back toward the dominant-coalition norm until the next series of shocks.

Subsystem political change may be driven by any one of the preceding, but it is usually a result of the interaction of some combination of the factors mentioned.

It is useful to think of institutional conflict, party politics, and economic dislocation as independent variables, ideas or belief systems as intervening variables,
and subsystem participation as the dependent variable. Still, the relationship
among the three should not be thought of simply as one characterized by unidi-
rectional causality. That is, the interaction among the three is what explains the
dynamic of subsystem politics. Causality runs both ways. Who gets what, when,
and how is determined not only by the larger context that buffets and shapes subsystem politics (so-called macrolevel variables) but also by the interaction of
members, would-be members, and challengers of policy monopolies (microlevel
variables) and the interaction of both with mesolevel variables (beliefs and ideas)
(see Figure 1.1).

PREVIEW OF BOOK

Subsystems are an equilibrium solution of a sort to the dilemma presented by interest group politics. A major problem associated with group politics is the seeming inability to effect closure on decisions that affect large numbers of interests.
Subsystems simply restrict the number of interested parties involved in policy-

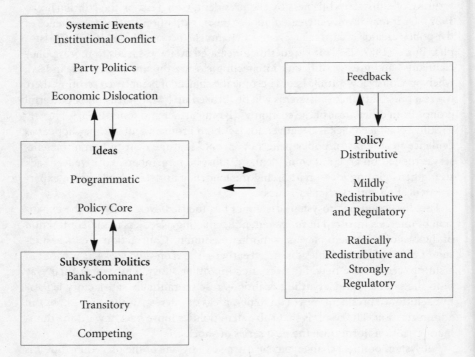

FIGURE 1.1   Explaining subsystem political change

making, greatly simplifying the deal cutting that occurs during formulation. They do so through the creation of institutional and intellectual barriers to participation in the policy process. Yet such barriers are not impermeable (Riker 1980; Krehbiel 1991). Indeed, the preceding section suggested that a variety of environmental forces outside the subsystem, as well as internal dynamics within a subsystem, provide a constant set of challenges to subsystem-induced equilibrium.

Rather than viewing subsystems as a general-equilibrium solution, I suggest that variation in subsystem politics represents a wavering equilibrium. The notion of a wavering equilibrium recognizes that although policy monopolies represented by subsystems may indeed be unstable (Baumgartner and Jones 1993, 5), the instability need not produce the end of such arrangements. Rather, politics wavers, moving away from the dominant-coalition norm toward more open arrangements, back toward dominant coalitions, and so on, in a never-ending minuet of bargaining, deal cutting, and politicking.

In this study I am interested in answering three interrelated questions with regard to the wavering equilibrium in the financial subsystem. First, what have been the major patterns of participation, or political variation, in the financial subsystem for the first approximately 100 years of its existence? Second, what accounts for those patterns and the change from one type of politics to another? Finally, what are the consequences of different types of subsystem politics for public policy? That is, how does the change in participation affect the legislative process, the content of legislation, and the identity of beneficiaries of legislation?

The first task of this study is to develop the means of constructing a portrait of the financial subsystem through time that allows one to highlight the dynamism of financial regulatory politics. To borrow a metaphor from Christopher Bosso (1987), most studies of the policy process present one with a series of unfinished canvases. The trick is to unite the various works so as to present a more complete and compelling portrait. Subsystem politics are dynamic, but they are not chaotic. The preceding literature review indicates, and several students of policy suggest, that subsystem politics vary between identifiable forms (Hamm 1986 and 1987; Bosso 1987; McCool 1989 and 1990). The identity of key interests is a principal distinguishing feature of the different forms of politics. Table 1.1 constructs a continuum of subsystem politics bounded by dominant coalitions on one end and competitive coalitions on the other.

Table 1.1 presents the variety of subsystem flora that populate the political landscape. All exhibit a tendency to restrict participation, produce policy that favors the few over the many, and limit policy outcomes to those desired by participants—in short to insulate subsystem members from the larger sociopolitical environment. Yet each varies in its ability to realize this goal. In order to get at this variation, this study examines the evolution of subsystem arrangements in a single policy area—financial regulation—over a period of roughly 100 years.

The study uses a combination of case studies and more abstract empirical measures to capture the dynamic of subsystem politics. The case-study chapters

TABLE 1.1   Three Models of Subsystem Politics

	Dominant	*Transitory*	*Competing*
Principal players	Legislators from oversight committee, regulators, and the regulated	Preceding players, president, academics, idea entrepreneurs, and experts	Players from several subsystems and other well-organized interests
Number and variety of interests	Small & narrow	Moderate	Moderate & varied
Frequency of appearance	Regular	Infrequent	Regular
Access	Closed	Somewhat open	Open
Basis of challenge	Economic	Economic, shared knowledge	Different policy beliefs, knowledge, economic
Decisionmaking autonomy	High	High to moderate	Moderate to low
Politics	Consensual	Entrepreneurial	Conflictual
Policy type	Distributive	Mildly redistributive & regulatory	Radically redistributive & regulatory

highlight the variables that constantly buffet and often alter subsystem politics. As such, they focus on factors that contribute to the expansion and contraction of the variety of interests involved in the financial subsystem during select periods. The case studies allow one to examine the dynamics of subsystem politics in a fairly detailed fashion by focusing on important institutional and ideational foundations of the financial subsystem. The more abstract empirical chapters allow one to view macrolevel change in politics over a longer time frame. They also detail the results of such change on the legislative activities and policy outputs of the financial subsystem over time. Throughout the book, I develop and employ a means of tracing change in subsystem politics that highlights the variables that contribute to change and allows one to observe the policy results of political variation.

Chapter 2 sets the stage for the study, offering a brief history of financial regulation beginning with the story of the passage of the Federal Reserve Act and ending with the passage of New Deal financial regulation. Tracing the development of the Federal Reserve allows one to document the birth and development of the financial subsystem. The chapter demonstrates the essential role of ideas in creating the bonds that allowed the variety of players involved in the financial sector to speak and think of themselves as members of a subsystem.

Chapter 3 develops a congressionally based empirical measure of subsystem politics. The measure allows one to classify the politics of financial regulation for any particular session of Congress as symptomatic of dominant, transitory, or competing coalitions. The chapter maps the financial subsystem terrain over the course of seventy years, giving one a feel for the changing nature of subsystem politics.

Chapter 4 focuses on the dynamics of the legislative process in the House and Senate. Care is taken to demonstrate how change in subsystem politics affects the routine of each of the banking committees, as well as the other committees dealing with financial regulation. Several studies have illustrated how a change in routine, rules, or procedures in Congress can impact the type of policy produced or considered (Oppenheimer 1975; Bosso 1987). This chapter explores this possibility in each of the chambers.

Chapter 5 traces the beneficiaries of financial regulation over the course of seventy years. Using the classificatory schema developed in Chapter 3, it illustrates variation in beneficiaries based on subsystem politics. Chapters 6 and 7 contain case studies that illustrate the dynamics of politics in the financial subsystem in greater detail. Chapter 6 traces the development of bank holding-company regulation in the period from 1933 to 1955. The bank holding-company case allows one to observe the policy process as it unfolds in a competitive setting and is eventually resolved under bank-dominant conditions. Chapter 7 documents how politics change when the system is under extreme duress, focusing on the attempt to deregulate the financial industry in the 1980s under competitive-coalition conditions. The final chapter returns to the question of politics and policy with which the study began.

The Birth and Evolution of the Financial Subsystem: A Historical Overview, 1865–1935

Financial regulation has been a hot topic of debate since the mid-1980s. A series of problems plaguing the thrift industry, together with related difficulties in commercial banking, have forced the financial industry, financial regulators, and select legislators into the limelight. Widespread public scrutiny of the financial industry of the type associated with the savings and loan debacle of the 1980s and 1990s, or the bank crisis of the 1990s, is relatively rare. When it comes to financial regulation, the norm is for business to be conducted by those intimately connected to the enterprise with as little outside involvement as possible.

Who are these players and how did they gain this power? The bulk of this chapter is concerned with answering the latter part of this question. But before turning to the historical development of the financial subsystem, I offer a preview of the principal players. The following section contains a brief glimpse of the primary financial intermediaries—commercial banks, thrifts, credit unions—and their regulatory counterparts.

THE FINANCIAL SUBSYSTEM: A PREVIEW OF THE PLAYERS

Commercial Banks

Commercial banks are what most of us think of when the topic of banking comes up. Commercial banks accept deposits and offer loans, traditionally in the form of short-term notes to business. Commercial banks are among the most numerous species of financial intermediary, numbering 10,450 with nearly 45,000 branches controlling $4,170,710 million in assets (Federal Deposit Insurance Corporation [hereafter FDIC] 1996). Most commercial banks are organized as stock companies, a feature that in the past distinguished them from thrifts (Meier 1985).

Banking interests are well organized. Two trade associations represent their interests: The American Bankers Association (ABA) is the original peak association that represents the industry as a whole; the Independent Bankers Association of America (IBAA) is a more recent creation, formed specifically to represent the interests of smaller institutions.

Financial regulation in the United States is unique in that it is conducted by two levels of government. The dual-banking system offers most financial intermediaries a choice of state or national chartering and regulatory authorities. In the case of commercial banking, regulatory authority at the national level is further split among three agencies—the Office of the Comptroller of the Currency (OCC), the Federal Reserve (Fed), and the Federal Deposit Insurance Corporation (FDIC).

The OCC, an agency within the Treasury Department, was expressly developed to regulate the banking industry. The OCC was formed as part of the National Currency Act in 1863 and given increased powers by the Bank Act of 1865. The comptroller is responsible for the chartering of national banks as well as the conduct of examinations and the enforcement of select consumer-protection provisions.

The Federal Reserve system, or Fed, was created by the Federal Reserve Act of 1913. The system consists of twelve Reserve banks and a seven-member board of governors. The Reserve banks are member organizations that all nationally chartered banks are required to join. Member banks subscribe to the stock of individual Reserve banks, are required to keep a set amount of reserves on deposit at the Reserve bank in their district, and use their Reserve bank to clear checks, borrow funds, and take advantage of a variety of additional services that aid them in the conduct of their business. The board of governors manages the system, engaging in both the formulation of monetary policy and the regulation of member banks. Members of the board are appointed to staggered fourteen-year terms by the president, subject to Senate confirmation, and can be removed only through impeachment.

The Federal Deposit Insurance Corporation (FDIC) is a government corporation that insures the deposits of national banks. In addition to national banks, the vast majority of state-chartered banks (over 96 percent of deposits) are also insured by the FDIC. The principal regulatory roles of the FDIC are to ensure the soundness of state-chartered banks receiving insurance and to issue cease-and-desist orders in the case of improper management by insured banks (national and state). The FDIC is governed by a three-member board that includes the comptroller and two members appointed for six-year terms by the president.

Savings and Loans

Thrifts, or savings and loans, were designed for a single purpose—to aid those interested in purchasing a home. Thrifts attracted long-term savers, at least before 1970, and financed long-term mortgages for the purchase of homes. Before the demise of Regulation Q in the 1980s, thrifts were allowed by law to offer a higher rate of return on deposits than commercial banks, in effect carving out a market for deposits through regulation. There are 1,459 thrifts with 9,402 branches in the United States with assets just under $771 billion (FDIC 1996).

Most thrifts belong to the U.S. League of Savings Associations (USLSA) with additional associations such as the National League of Insured Savings Associations (NLISA) and a variety of state-level groups often joining the fray. In addition to being allied with industry trade associations, thrifts often form ties with the housing industry, cooperative associations, and the like. This latter feature illustrates an interesting difference between thrifts and banks: The former are closely tied to the clientele they were designed to serve—homeowners and the housing industry.

Until 1989 the Federal Home Loan Bank Board (FHLBB) was the thrift industry equivalent of the Federal Reserve. All nationally chartered savings and loans and mutual savings banks were members; state membership was optional. The FHLBB offered deposit insurance through the Federal Savings and Loan Insurance Corporation (FSLIC), whose stock was subscribed to by member institutions. The FHLBB also chartered thrifts, regulated all insured institutions, conducted examinations of members, and operated the Federal Home Loan Mortgage Corporation, which bought and sold home mortgages (Meier 1985, 43–44). Like the FDIC, the FHLBB was governed by a three-person board nominated by the president and confirmed by the Senate. Following the massive failure of thrifts in the 1980s and the bankrupting of the FSLIC, the FHLBB was reformed as the Office of Thrift Supervision (see Chapter 7).

Credit Unions

Credit unions by law are depository institutions that serve a select group of individuals based on a common bond of employment, association, or residence (Meier 1985, 39). Most are associated with an employer. Members technically purchase shares (deposits) in the credit union and make loans to members. Most credit unions are small-time operations; 12,174 credit unions control assets of $330 billion (FDIC 1996).

The National Credit Union Administration (NCUA) was established in 1970 to charter federal credit unions, operate an insurance fund—the National Credit Union Share Insurance Fund—and regulate all those institutions subscribing to the insurance fund. The NCUA is governed by a three-person board appointed by the president and approved by the Senate.

The financial subsystem, then, is a hodgepodge of public and private actors. The exotic mix of regulators and regulated makes the policy process complex even during the most mundane of times. During crises it may appear downright chaotic, at least on the surface. Despite the seemingly untidy mix of actors, the financial subsystem operates in a fairly orderly manner. Why this is so has to do with the very nature of subsystem arrangements, a subject we now turn to in greater detail.

THE BIRTH AND MATURATION OF
THE (SUB)SYSTEM IDEAL

Most observers of the subsystem phenomenon overlook the birth of subsystems, preferring to observe them in action or track their demise. Perhaps this is because many associate the subsystem phenomenon with the New Deal, or as Theodore Lowi characterized it, "the Second Republic of the United States" (1969). In detailing the rise of "interest group liberalism," which culminated in the institutionalization of the positive state, Lowi seemed to settle the debate over when the subsystem phenomenon entered onto the American political scene. This chapter does not so much challenge Lowi's account of the growth of the positive state as much as it argues over the date, and some of the circumstances, of its birth. The groundwork for subsystem arrangements in banking was laid as far back as the Civil War, took shape during the latter part of the Progressive era, and reached maturity during the New Deal. The New Deal marked the institutionalization of subsystem arrangements along lines that would exist virtually unchanged for nearly sixty years, and the circumstances leading up to the adoption of New Deal financial regulation should not be neglected. The early history of financial regulation details the forces that led to the birth of the financial subsystem and also explains why subsystem politics vary through time.

Financial regulation has been shaped by a relatively small number of legislative acts. The regulatory structure established by the Currency Act of 1863 and the National Bank Act of 1864 remained virtually unchanged until the passage of the Federal Reserve Act in 1913. The new regulatory setup was itself in a state of flux until the 1930s, when New Deal banking regulation resolved significant jurisdictional questions left unanswered by the Federal Reserve Act. The Federal Reserve Act, and the New Deal amendments to the act, established the institutional relationships and core ideas that still serve as the basis of the financial subsystem.

The early history of financial regulation, then, is the story of the birth and development of the financial subsystem. Until banks thought of themselves as part of a system or enterprise markedly different from other business endeavors, there was no shared sense of purpose and interest, which lies at the heart of subsystem arrangements. Not only must banks share this belief, they must be joined in it by regulators and legislators who enshrine the beliefs in institutions such as law, regulatory practice, committee jurisdiction, and regulatory organizations. The activity leading up to the passage of the Federal Reserve Act was an important step in this direction. As such it is best viewed as institution building in action.

In tracing the evolution of financial regulation, I pay special attention to the identity of interests, taking note of any efforts to restrict participation and influence; ideas, principally those that guide attempts to create a financial system via regulation; and institutions and the manner in which they shape and are shaped by the activities of key subsystem players and events over time. In focusing on the periods of greatest regulatory change—the years leading up to the passage of the

Federal Reserve Act through the passage of New Deal regulation—one is examining instances in which the financial system itself is in turmoil. As such, the period leading up to the institutionalization of the Federal Reserve system serves as a case study in how external variables shape subsystem politics, providing the dynamic that explains, in part, policy outcomes in the financial subsystem.

THE ORIGINS OF THE FEDERAL RESERVE SYSTEM

Historically, the periods of greatest debate concerning reform of the financial regulatory structure occur during the various instances of panic and failure that regularly plague banking in the United States (West 1977, 36).[1] Financial and economic instability associated with the variety of banknotes in circulation and the difficulty in redemption was a major force behind the passage of the Currency Act of 1863 and the National Bank Act of 1864 (Hammond 1957; Trescott 1963; Robertson 1968). The underlying policy core beliefs and their programmatic incarnations as enshrined in the currency and bank acts are displayed in Table 2.1.

The currency and bank acts created a single, uniform currency backed by national government bonds (bond-secured notes), set up the Office of the Comptroller of the Currency (OCC) to oversee the chartering of national banks, and issued a set of standards (including reserve requirements) intent on promoting the soundness of national banks (see Table 2.1). The fundamental underlying principle of the acts was that banking should be open to all qualified applicants, something the chartering authority would ensure. Of equal importance was the belief that financial power should not be concentrated in the hands of the few, another goal to be pursued via regulation.

The acts were the first attempt to create a national system of government-regulated private banks. Yet the currency and bank acts fell short of creating a financial *system*, due in large part to the resistance of banking interests, a lack of consensus

TABLE 2.1   The National Bank System, 1863–1913

Policy Core Beliefs	Programmatic Incarnations
Normative	
1. Banking should be open to all qualified comers.	1. Clearing houses and reserve city banks as quasi-regulators
Empirical	2. Control of issuance of bank notes
1. Regulation should be accomplished through chartering.	3. Charter granting
2. Dual chartering should be divided between state regulators and the Office of the Comptroller.	4. Capitalization requirements
3. All qualified applicants should be granted a charter.	

over what constituted regulation, and the underdeveloped nature of the institutions necessary to anchor the system ideal in the rough and tumble world of nineteenth-century industrial capitalism.

The currency and bank acts were a potential institutional basis for the development of a financial system, but they did not create a system through the mere act of their passage. Part of this was due to the nature of the acts themselves. Despite the announced intention of the acts to create sound banks and a stable currency, the immediate goal of the acts was not primarily regulatory. Passed during the Civil War, the Currency Act in particular was designed to meet one objective, raising revenue for the Union war effort. Thus although a regulatory element was introduced by the acts, neither bill did much in the way of creating an agency capable of regulating the activity of financial institutions. The OCC was but one chartering authority available to those interested in the business of banking, and an underfunded and understaffed one at that. State authorities were still allowed to charter banks, giving rise to a dual-banking system that hindered the stringency of regulatory enforcement by the comptroller.

As a result, banking in the latter half of the nineteenth century was still characterized by regular periods of panic and failure—as were all business enterprises (Hammond 1957; West 1977; White 1983). By the turn of the century several factors came together that made it increasingly difficult to view the periodically recurring bank failures as part of the normal cost of doing business.

Explaining Bank Failures:
Regulation as Systems Management

The process of reinterpreting bank failure as a problem suitable for government attention went through two stages. Discussion moved from a preoccupation with currency problems to a focus on the organization of the banking system itself (West 1977, 35). Initial reform discussions, dominated by the Treasury and the OCC, were sparked by the panic of 1873, in which widespread bank failure threw the economy into a minor depression. Two problems in particular stood out: the payment of interests on reserves and the general condition of currency inelasticity (the shortage of currency during particular periods of the business year).[2]

The secretary of the Treasury and the comptroller were joined in the reform discussion by the New York Clearing House Committee (NYCHC). The NYCHC served as a "central bank" for New York City financial institutions, clearing drafts, informally setting interest rates, and policing the competition among banks in the city. All agreed that the payment of interest on reserves and the resulting speculation by reserve banks were key variables contributing to, and exacerbating, the 1873 crisis (Office of the Comptroller 1872 and 1873; Department of the Treasury 1873). There was less consensus on a solution to the problem.

Although nothing legislative came from the reform discussions, they are significant for two reasons. First, they were restricted to a select group of interests—

public and private regulators—a hallmark of subsystem politics. In addition, the entrance of national regulatory authorities on the scene was a marked change from the immediate past. Indeed, regulators took the initiative, suggesting ways of broadening their powers so as to both control individual bank practice and alleviate systemic problems that affected banking. The proposals by the comptroller indicate the OCC had taken on a new mission, which although perhaps implicit since its establishment, was now given explicit form—the prevention of panics and failures among nationally chartered institutions.

Second, both public and private actors viewed the problems plaguing banks from a systems perspective. That is, implicit in the discussion of the public and private regulators was the notion that the problems of currency inelasticity and the payment of interests on reserves were problems facing all banks. The systems notion was still in its infancy, but it was an important step away from the free-banking ethos enshrined in the National Bank Act. The discussion of the problem by regulators recognized that banks performed a function that was markedly different from business, that they could not and should not operate on laissez-faire principles applicable to other forms of economic endeavor. In short, banking was a business that required regulation.

The fact that nothing came of the reform proposals highlights the significant, indeed dominant, role of the financial industry in the process. Even as a "non-player," the financial industry was able to block the extension of regulation, which most banks still viewed as unnecessary interference. Still, the events of 1873 hint at the outlines of the financial subsystem—dominated by the interests of the financial industry but also shaped by the goals of regulators—slowly emerging out of the primordial setting of late-nineteenth-century industrial America.

Regulatory Reform: The Banks Join In

Following another panic in 1893, there was a distinct change in the emphasis of reform proposals within the banking community. Discussion among bankers shifted from a focus on individual banking practice and mismanagement as the cause of failures and panics to systemic explanations of failure. The seeds of this line of reasoning had been apparent in the remarks of the secretary of the Treasury and the comptroller of the currency two decades earlier; this argument was now taken up by bankers as well. Debate focused on problems associated with the circulation of currency (*Banker* 1893; Mints 1945, 198–206; West 1977, 42–43).[3] Most of the financial industry was in agreement on the causes of panics and failures—a lack of currency during particular periods of the business cycle and the need for a new system of currency issue. The exact form the system would take sparked a good deal of debate. Banks were divided into three factions: New York City banks, Midwestern urban banks, and small-town and rural "unit" banks.

Two vehicles served as the focus of reform discussion in the banking community. The first came out of the American Bankers Association annual convention in Baltimore in 1894. The ABA, dominated by urban midwestern banks, issued its Baltimore Plan, which established a new currency based on bank assets and created a "guarantee fund" intended to secure the soundness of the new currency. The fund, organized and run by the member banks, would be used to redeem the notes of insolvent banks during crises.[4]

The Baltimore Plan clearly borrowed its explanation for currency inelasticity from the Treasury and OCC models proposed some twenty years earlier. Yet just as clearly it sought a private, bank-controlled solution to the problem of currency inelasticity, going so far as to advocate the removal of the few vestiges of government regulation—bond-secured note issues—that characterized the national regulatory structure. Even though the plan was bank authored and supported by leading bankers in Chicago and Milwaukee, it generated opposition from most of the banking community. New York City banks viewed it as a power play by the midwestern banks. Rural banks decried the failure of the plan to recognize rural assets as appropriate backing for currency (White 1983, 84).

Following closely on the heels of the Baltimore Plan, an alliance of bankers, academics, and the nonfinancial industry tried its hand at regulatory reform. The Indianapolis Monetary Commission assembled members of the newly emerging corporate class in pursuit of reform quite similar to that enunciated in Baltimore four years earlier.[5] Although few actors with official government ties were at the conference, Treasury secretary Lyman Gage did offer his support to the commission. The Indianapolis gathering proposed a solution quite similar to the Baltimore Plan, adding a role for nonbanking industry interests in the administration of the system. Like its Baltimore cousin, the Indianapolis Plan received a chilly response from most of the banking community outside the Midwest. Still, it made an imprint on one important player—New Jersey's Charles N. Fowler, the Republican chair of the House Committee on Banking and Currency (West 1977, 46; Livingston 1986).

Completing the Circle: Congress Joins the Fray

Although system-oriented solutions were kicked around by important banking and industry interests at the Baltimore and Indianapolis meetings, little in the way of concrete progress occurred. To be sure, moving the discussion to a systems perspective was an important alteration in ideas, but breathing life into the dream required action by an authoritative actor. Banking still spoke with too many voices. The role of entrepreneur fell to Charles Fowler.

Fowler first introduced legislation based on the ideas enunciated at the Indianapolis and Baltimore meetings in 1902. By introducing legislation in the House, Fowler moved the process from a forum controlled by the banking industry to a setting in which additional players might join the fray. In this fashion he reclaimed a role for the House Banking Committee by allying himself with the midwestern reform forces.

It was five years before Fowler, in response to the panic of 1907, was able to shepherd another bill through the House Banking Committee. This time, however, Fowler was not the only government actor who attempted to assume the role of entrepreneur. Democratic presidential hopeful William Jennings Bryan was pushing a reform scheme of his own, and the GOP responded accordingly. With all this activity it was only a matter of time before the real power in banking— New York City banks and trust operations—stepped into the fray. New York City banks began a campaign to take control of the ABA and the course of reform discussions in the early years of the twentieth century. Their vehicle of choice was the Currency Commission of the New York Chamber of Commerce.

The New York City banks' solution to the problem of currency inelasticity was the creation of a central bank (Wiebe 1963). Frank Vanderlip, a former Treasury official and New York City banker, was the intellectual force in the Chamber of Commerce. The Currency Commission formed the nucleus of a network of policy experts that took on a critical mass around the turn of the century. At the core of the commission were some of the leading lights of the economics and political science movements at America's leading universities. Worried by the antics of Bryan, distrustful of the midwestern bankers it viewed as upstarts, the new coalition of business, academics, and bankers worked to define the problems facing the financial industry as a technical rather than a political issue (Livingston 1986, 165–176).

Demonstrating the depth of animosity that separated the midwestern reformers from their New York City brethren, Vanderlip dismissed the House Banking Committee as "practically without influence" (Livingston 1986, 181). The New York City–led reform coalition looked instead to the Senate Banking Committee as the vehicle through which to realize its goals. The coalition response to the Fowler plan was enshrined in a bill introduced in the Senate by the Republican majority leader from Rhode Island, Nelson Aldrich, following consultation with J. P. Morgan and other powerful New York City financial interests (Wiebe 1963, 72–73).

Clearly favoring the major money-center banks in New York City, the Aldrich bill alienated a sizable portion of the financial community. Passed by the Senate, it received a cold reception in the House. Fowler had been written off by New York City bankers as irrelevant, but he still enjoyed the backing of midwestern bankers. In a leadership-led coup, Republican Speaker of the House Joseph Cannon removed Fowler from the chairmanship of the Banking Committee. This opened the door for Representative Edward Vreeland, a Banking Committee Republican from upstate New York, to introduce a White House–backed compromise measure in the House. With the backing of the Speaker, the bill was passed in the House and sent to the Senate. Signed into law in mid-May 1908, Aldrich-Vreeland recognized any securities held by banks as acceptable collateral for an emergency currency, designated private banks engaged in clearing house operations as overseers during crises, and created the National Monetary Commission (NMC) to study the need for more comprehensive reform and act as the ultimate arbiter of the act (Livingston 1986, 187).

Aldrich-Vreeland began to unravel almost as soon as it was passed—due in no small part to the split between midwestern and New York City banks. In addition, corporate capital, small business, and agricultural interests all sought a more stable source of funding—something the act was unable to provide. The problem was that proposals for a centralized control mechanism—public, private, or hybrid— were a direct challenge to those who were against the centralization of authority. Similarly, the system notion itself qualified beliefs concerning the sanctity of the dual-banking structure. Finally, the unit-banking ideal—that banking should be open to all interested parties with as few strings attached as possible—was potentially threatened by increased regulation.

Still, demands for system reform raised presidential interest in restructuring banking. Forces within and outside the financial community worked in combination to force the issue of a central bank back on the agenda. Debate centered on two topics: the shape of the system (centralized versus decentralized) and control of the system (public versus private) (West 1977).

One More Time: The NMC Takes Charge

A good deal of the debate over the shape of the new regulatory arrangements took place under the auspices of the National Monetary Commission (NMC). Created by Aldrich-Vreeland to study the need for more comprehensive reform and act as the ultimate arbiter of the act, the NMC was viewed by the New York City faction of the ABA as a necessary precaution "to keep the financial issue out of politics." The commission—chaired by Senator Aldrich—was the forum for discussion among members of the House and Senate Banking Committees. "My idea," Aldrich told his House counterpart, Theodore Burton, "is, of course, that everything shall be done in the most quiet manner possible and without any public announcement" (Livingston 1986, 188). The commission was intent on keeping the reform discussion restricted to a tight circle of participants in the early stages of the process. Select academics, money-center bankers, representatives of corporate capital, and a handful of legislators from the Banking Committees in both chambers were involved in the "collection of facts" leading up to the announcement of a reform agenda.[6] As such, the NMC was a perfect example of subsystem policymaking.

The NMC proposed the creation of a new regulatory body that mixed elements of public and private control. The outgrowth of the NMC proposal was introduced in the Senate in 1911. The Aldrich Plan, as it was known, proposed the creation of a system—the National Reserve Association—that served as the blueprint for the Federal Reserve system. The system was to be owned by the banks that subscribed to its stock with a head office in Washington and fifteen regional branches. It was headed by a forty-five-member National Reserve Board dominated by bankers and businessmen with six ex officio members appointed by the president. All nationally chartered banks were eligible for membership in the association with no changes in operation required of them. State-chartered institutions were required to meet capital and reserve requirements of the National Banking Act.

The banking system envisioned in the Aldrich bill reflected the distaste for government regulation and the fear of centralization of control, which pervaded banking. There was little role for public actors in the plan; it was run primarily by bankers with some input from industrial and commercial interests. The manner in which the board was chosen favored smaller banks, and the system envisioned was clearly based on the clearinghouse principle as practiced in New York (West 1977, 73). The chances for passage of the Aldrich Plan dwindled as the presidential election neared. The split within the Republican party between the Taft wing and the Roosevelt insurgents, combined with the candidacy of Woodrow Wilson for the Democrats, sidetracked presidential support for reform. In addition, the Pujo Committee's investigation of the "money trust" cast suspicion on any reform backed by New York City financial interests (Wiebe 1963, 78).

The Federal Reserve Act

Although the election of 1912 produced Democratic control of Congress and the White House, the bill that came out of the House banking subcommittee looked remarkably like the Republican-produced Aldrich proposal of the previous session. Much of the similarity had to do with the relatively unchanged roster of players involved in formulation, in particular the nature of the "expert" advice the new majority members of the House Banking Committee received.

The policy expert attached to the House banking subcommittee, Henry Parker Willis, a professor at Washington and Lee as well as a financial writer for the *Journal of Commerce*, had strong ties to the NMC. Willis was the intellectual driving force behind a banking subcommittee that had few members with any banking experience or background. He tutored the members, including committee chair Carter Glass of Virginia, on banking theory through a number of forums—public hearings, private sessions before the hearings began, position papers, and the like—sending the Democratic members of the Banking Committee to the NMC school of central banking. Any questions left unanswered during their tutorial with Willis were answered by the testimony of regulators and regulated, which remained fairly consistent with that given during the Aldrich bill deliberations. The parallels between the Glass and Aldrich bills were so strong that the House Banking Committee, in an analytical summary of the bill it eventually brought to the floor as the Federal Reserve Act, admitted, "The objects technically aimed at [in the Aldrich Plan] were desirable" with the only question left to work on "the methods by which . . . to carry them out" (Livingston 1986, 216). The result was a reform measure that emphasized divisional reserve banks under joint public-private control much like its predecessor, but with an important twist. After consultation with President Woodrow Wilson, Willis and Glass agreed to add an oversight board to their plan. The addition of what would become the Federal Reserve Board introduced an added degree of tension to the proceedings that followed.

Although the seeming continuity between the Aldrich and Glass proposals should have smoothed the waters stirred by the transition from Republican to Democratic government, the manner in which Glass and Willis managed the process—freezing out Republican members of the Banking Committee—only served to aggravate the situation. The addition of a Federal Reserve Board stocked with presidential appointees and charged with system oversight worried Republican legislators, many bankers, and some of the principal architects of the Aldrich Plan. A common theme of the complaints concerned the opportunity for "outsider" participation, portrayed as meddling by nonbankers, in the workings of the business of finance. In response to the complaints, Glass staggered the terms of board members so that no single president could control the board. In addition, the Reserve banks themselves were to be controlled by the financial industry, adding yet another barrier to potential outsider involvement (Livingston 1986, 220–223; West 1977).

The passage of the Federal Reserve Act introduced new institutional players into the financial subsystem—the various Reserve banks and the Federal Reserve Board. The act itself was the institutional embodiment of the idea that banks and banking were part of a system that was totally unlike other forms of economic enterprise (see Table 2.2). It developed a system of governance that was a hybrid

TABLE 2.2   The Federal Reserve System, 1913–1933

Policy Core Beliefs	*Programmatic Incarnations*
Normative	
1. Industry must be preserved.	1. Federal Reserve requirements
2. Concentration of power is bad.	2. Charter granting
3. Markets require correction.	3. Capitalization requirements
4. Currency management is necessary.	
5. Banks are a special kind of business enterprise.	
Empirical	
1. Currency flow must be controlled.	
2. Dual regulation should be divided between state and national regulators.	
3. Regulation should be split among the OCC, Federal Reserve Board, Federal Reserve banks, Treasury, and clearing house banks.	

of public and private regulation. And yet, although the act was an explicit recognition by all involved of the unique role of banks and banking in the economy and polity, it still left the question of control unresolved. That is, control was vested in the system, but the question of who controlled the system was left unanswered.

The vague statutory language of the Federal Reserve Act created tension between the Federal Reserve Board and Reserve banks concerning the proper conduct, and source, of monetary and banking policy. The board, created at the insistence of President Wilson, was resented by both the banking community and Carter Glass. Both saw it as a thinly veiled attempt to centralize control over banking, an executive intrusion into the financial subsystem.

The problem of control was exacerbated by a division between the House and Senate over the type of system created by the Federal Reserve Act. The debate prior to the passage of the act reveals the House believed it created a decentralized system, in keeping with the intent of Carter Glass. The Senate just as clearly insisted the act created a centralized system. This difference of intent did little to settle the dispute between the board and the Reserve banks. To further complicate matters, the Treasury made a claim to power based upon a passage in the Federal Reserve Act that seemed to reserve certain broadly defined powers to it. The intrusion of the Treasury into the day-to-day affairs of the subsystem was interpreted as another attempt by the president to gain control over financial regulation, further magnifying the tension concerning the locus of power in the Federal Reserve system. Banks immediately sided with the Reserve banks in their struggle with the board. The Treasury took a similar tack, perhaps sensing a rival in the board and choosing to deal with the Reserve banks on questions of monetary policy. The result was that the regulatory role of the Federal Reserve was effectively neutralized by a three-way struggle for power among the Reserve banks, the board, and the Treasury, which was not settled until 1935 (West 1977, 213–226).

The passage of the Federal Reserve Act was an important first step toward the creation of a banking system. Still, the implementation of the act fell short of institutionalizing a coherent financial subsystem ethos. Much of this had to do with the vague commitment of the financial industry, regulators, and legislators to different variations of the system ideal. Some held to the central-banking model; others clung to a government-sanctioned clearinghouse ideal.[7] One faction argued the system was simply a stopgap to be used in emergencies; others saw in it a tool for constant management of the money and credit supply. Finally, there was the debate over the locus of authority in the system—with most favoring the Reserve banks but some arguing for the preeminence of the board. In short, although the notion of a "system" had entered the vocabulary of most members of the financial community, it was still fairly amorphous, evident from the lack of agreement on the programmatic realization of the system ideal. The outbreak of World War I and the use of government controls on credit and industry, followed by the boom of the 1920s, put off the need for settling the quandary. It was not until the stock market crash of 1929 and the ensuing banking and business disaster that the system question was finally settled.[8]

The passage of the Federal Reserve Act represents the birth of the financial subsystem. Events leading up to the passage of the act foreshadow the important role of systemic variables in shaping and sustaining subsystem politics. Most notable was the effect of economic downturns, the boom and bust cycle of early capitalism, and bank panics that followed. Clearly the architects of the new banking system were acting to alleviate the downside of laissez-faire. The original impetus behind the Federal Reserve Act was to erect a panic-proof banking system. Similarly, party politics helped to move the reform discussion along. Democrats, egged on by William Jennings Bryan and the Populists, added bank reform to their platform. Republicans, the original party of reform allied with Progressives in the Midwest, kept the reform question alive. And lest we forget, it was a Democratic president, Woodrow Wilson, who in large measure shaped the Federal Reserve system through his addition of a board of governors. Finally, as emphasized in the preceding section, ideas played a major role in shaping and giving life to the system ideal. Indeed, it was the lack of clear consensus on important core principles and programmatic elements in the 1920s that led to disaster in the 1930s, as the following section details.

INSTITUTIONALIZING THE SYSTEM: THE NEW DEAL REFORMS

In historical perspective the depression assumes a monumental scale, but in reading through contemporary accounts of the events one is struck time and again by the inability of many of the key players to recognize the magnitude of the problem. Much of this unawareness had to do with the ideas that shaped the dominant paradigm of players both within and outside the financial subsystem. Actors in the financial subsystem interpreted the events of 1929 as simply another panic. Having erected a system via the Federal Reserve that was immune to major damage, or so they believed, they were trapped in this perception and proved unable to understand and handle the crisis.

The initial response to the wave of bank failures took three forms. The first was a financial industry–led effort to devise a private-sector solution to the problem, with Republican president Herbert Hoover participating in a peripheral fashion. Following closely on the heels of this initiative was the construction of a quasi-public response by the Federal Reserve Board—the Reconstruction Finance Corporation (RFC). A final, mostly private, solution involved the creation of banking-industrial committees by the various Federal Reserve banks. Both the RFC and banking-industrial committees provided a bridge between advocates of a wholly private solution and those calling for increased government involvement. In the end, all three proved unable to resolve the problem of panic and increased failure of financial institutions. What they did do was provide feedback to key players outside the subsystem that convinced them something had to be done. In this fashion, the failure of the newly developed "panic proof" system to remedy the situation forced a reassessment of several of the principal ideas on which the old system was based. The exercise in reassessment was systemwide, that is, it occurred throughout the polity and produced a new set of beliefs enshrined in the New Deal regulatory regime (Eisner 1993).

Bank-Authored Solutions

One of the first coalitions to form in response to the events of 1929 was a marriage of necessity between bankers and President Hoover. The president initiated a series of conferences between bankers and businessmen that resulted in the formation of the National Credit Corporation (NCC). The NCC had a war chest of $500 million made available by New York City banks, which was intended as an emergency fund for rediscounting notes of banks not eligible for Federal Reserve discounting.[9] The attempted resurrection of private clearinghouses vis-à-vis the NCC was the last gasp of the hard-core antiregulatory movement, as well as the last hurrah of those advocating a completely private solution to the problems of the depression. The wholly private attempt began to founder almost immediately when larger money-center banks proved reluctant (and unable) to bail out a sizable portion of failing institutions. Meanwhile, Hoover and the banking community continued to define the events of 1929 as just another round of failure and panic and waited for the newly institutionalized Federal Reserve to steady the system.

The Federal Reserve Board response to the crisis took the form of the RFC. The brainchild of Fed chair Eugene Meyer, the RFC was empowered "to make loans, on adequate collateral security, to industries, railroads, and financial institutions which could not otherwise secure credit" as long as the advances stimulated employment (Burns 1974, 15). President Hoover agreed to the RFC reluctantly, and only after the NCC market-like solution proved inadequate for dealing with the crisis. Directed by a board of seven members, including the secretary of the Treasury, and chaired by Eugene Meyer, the RFC was the last serious attempt to deal with the crisis that did not include a fundamental change in the existing regulatory structure. The RFC served as a bank for those interests banks refused to serve, and as such it was to be a temporary expedient until banker confidence could be restored.

While the Fed Board was experimenting with the RFC solution, the various Federal Reserve banks explored a solution of their own. They established banking-industrial committees in each Fed district in an effort to determine the credit needs of the district. The committees were to act as information clearinghouses, informing potential credit recipients of available sources of funds. Despite these efforts, little in the way of increased lending occurred in any of the districts. This was because the activities of the various Reserve banks suffered from a lack of co-ordination between districts. In addition, the banking members of the banking-industrial committees operated on the assumption that the problem of credit in-elasticity was secondary to the protection of sound banks' portfolios. Bankers preferred to approach the problem of tight money as a local one. The larger, sound banks, which dominated the committees, argued that generous (impru-dent) lending policies and overly concentrated portfolios were responsible for the string of failures plaguing many smaller institutions. In their view the proper so-lution to the problem was to allow market forces to run their course, or allow the failure of the nonprudent. The tight credit policy of the sound banks alienated not only small banks but bank customers, regulators, and elected officials.

As time passed, healthy banks showed little inclination to add to their loan portfolios, weaker institutions folded in record numbers, and the economy wors-ened. Although none of the preceding alone were conducive to the indirect in-volvement contemplated by the Fed and the president, their combined effect was disastrous.

Congressional Attempts to Police the Subsystem

If the president and much of the banking community seemed myopic in their devotion to a market-based approach, actions in Congress were only a slight im-provement. In the Senate, Carter Glass, now the Democratic senator from Vir-ginia, introduced the Banking Act of 1930 to serve as a guide in the Republican-controlled banking subcommittee's investigation of the crisis. Among the highlights of the Glass "guide" were provisions that removed the secretary of the Treasury from the Federal Reserve Board, allowed branch banking, and placed re-strictions on the security operations of national banks (for a more detailed treat-ment see Kennedy 1973; Burns 1974).

Only the latter provision was an attempt to get at the root cause of the rash of bank failures. Most subsystem players were more interested in settling an old score with regard to the Federal Reserve Board and presidential influence exer-cised through the board. Eliminating Treasury representation on the Federal Re-serve Board, although long sought by both Glass and much of the banking com-munity, had little to do with the causes of the crisis or with ameliorating its immediate effects. Rather it was an attempt to limit future presidential intrusion in subsystem affairs. The hope was that the removal of the Treasury position from the board would cut it off from its executive-branch base of support, mov-ing the struggle for power between the board and the various Federal Reserve branch banks closer to a solution favoring the latter. All the while the Reserve banks were proving themselves unable to deal with the crisis affecting banking.

Similarly, the debate over branching restrictions brought up an old bone of contention. To be sure, there was an argument that branching would strengthen the portfolios of small banks—the bulk of institutions that failed during crises—

by tying them into the diversified interests of larger institutions as branches. Even so, small banks feared the impact of increased competition, as did state banks and state regulators, all of whom argued against branching. The provision dealing with limits on securities operations sought the separation of investment banking from commercial banking. This was the most radical call for change, and one of the few attempts to actually limit what banks could do with depositors' funds.

For the most part, the Glass provisions quite simply sought to save banking as an industry. The changes in the structure of the Fed favored the banking industry, branching was a means of strengthening small banks through portfolio diversification, and securities restrictions forced prudent management on bank managers. As such, they were an attempt to save banks from themselves—something most banks resisted.

While the administration pursued the RFC route and the Senate entertained discussion of the Glass proposals, another topic inched its way onto the reform agenda. The predominate subject of the myriad of bank bills introduced in the Democrat-controlled House during 1932 was guaranteeing the safety of bank depositor funds through some type of deposit insurance. House Banking Committee chair Henry Steagall, Democrat of Alabama, introduced a deposit-insurance plan with the intention of attaching it to the Glass legislation when it arrived from the Senate. The opposition of banks and regulators to insurance schemes was nearly universal. Large banks, which had no problem meeting withdrawal requests, argued insurance would force them to underwrite the losses of smaller, less sound institutions. Not only that, deposit insurance was castigated as "subsidizing 'wild-cat management,'" which actually increased risk taking and the possibility of failure (Kennedy 1973, 216).

Small unit banks were split on the issue. State banks saw insurance as an attempt to force them into the national fold and resisted it accordingly. Nationally chartered unit banks tended to back insurance when faced with a choice between it or branching as a means of stabilizing the system. Still, most banks viewed insurance, and the cost of insurance premiums, as an unwelcome encroachment on portfolio decisions (*New York Times*, May 19, 1933; *Banker*, June 1933, 537–538 and 563–567). They were joined in opposition by the New York Federal Reserve Bank, which condemned insurance as "piecemeal tinkering," preferring a government guarantee against loss of select RFC loans (Burns 1974, 88–89). In addition, Senator Glass, President Hoover, and the Treasury all came out against insurance.

Deposit insurance, first suggested by House Banking Committee chair Charles N. Fowler at the turn of the century and experimented with by several states in the interim, was introduced to safeguard the interests of both banks and depositors. This latter goal, safeguarding depositor interests, distinguished the deposit-insurance proposal from the rest of the reform measures. Deposit insurance was originally suggested as a means of preventing depositor runs on sound institutions, but in the debate surrounding the issue, it was increasingly defined as a consumer-protection issue. Although it began as a subsystem-authored project, it was taken up by a variety of nonsubsystem interests soon after its introduction.

By 1932 the financial industry had proven itself unable to "grow out" of the banking crisis. Weathering the storm through tight credit policies might create a leaner, healthier banking industry in the long run, but the immediate costs were too high for banks faced with failure and for the wide variety of nonbanking interests caught up in the depression. The ability of the banking coalition to maintain control over the course of policy crumbled as market-based policies continued to take their toll. Banks hurt by the market approach, as well as business and industry suffering from tight credit policies, appealed to legislators, the president, and the public for a government-led solution to their problems. The Glass bill passed the Senate but was promptly shelved when it reached the House. The Steagall proposal passed the House only to be killed in the Senate. A growing coalition of nonsubsystem players challenged the right as well as the ability of banks to solve the crisis on their own. The failed attempt at an industry-coordinated solution in banking was simply one act in the larger drama unfolding in the economy as a whole.

A major problem was that the banking industry was still lined up against any increase in regulatory authority. The banking coalition as a force for positive action had clearly stalled following the failure of the two private attempts to deal with the crisis, yet they were still able to perform a blocking action of sorts. Inaction served the interests of the stronger members of the banking community, who were united in their opposition to the extension of federal regulation in any form.

Three events destroyed the banking-industry monopoly over the course of reform: the election of Democrat Franklin Roosevelt as president; the increasing number of bank failures and the declaration of the "bank holiday" in early March 1933; and a series of congressional hearings, also in March, that provided reformers with the leverage necessary to move the banking community toward acceptance of regulatory reform.

The Jig Is Up: The Pecora Hearings and New Deal Reforms

The presidential election of 1932 marked the end of the purely private, financial industry–dominated attempt to control the course of policy formulation. The Democratic landslide was a clear repudiation of previous efforts to deal with the depression. Interestingly enough, one of the first attempts to redefine the problems plaguing banking involved a congressional investigation of the stock market activities of select banks, requested by Hoover. The hearings, which began in 1932, culminated in a set of revelations in February 1933 during the lame duck session of Congress that set the stage for New Deal changes in the banking system.

The second half of the Senate investigation, known as the Pecora hearings, focused on the questionable ethics of select bankers, rendering a damning indictment of bankers and banks to which the public was quick to respond. One of the first stories to gain attention involved the former chairman of the RFC, Charles G. Dawes, who used the agency to float a loan to his bank after leaving the RFC. Although the loan itself was technically legal, it was necessary because of Dawes's inept handling of loans to the affiliates of the holding company that controlled his bank—loans that violated Illinois State banking law.

Pecora constructed a portrait of the RFC that suggested it was used to benefit the most powerful interests in the banking community while small banks and small businesses continued to fail in record numbers. In a masterful stroke he shattered the fragile unity of the bank coalition, playing on the growing split between large and small banks (Kennedy 1973, 40–42 and 104–128; Burns 1974, 22). The hearings turned into a series of revelations concerning the unscrupulous activities of bankers, whether they had anything to do with banking practice and the stock market or not. The point was quite simple: Bankers were of questionable moral character and should not be trusted with the public's life savings. The Pecora hearings were also an argument against self-regulation, suggesting that any solution in which banks played a major role was subject to manipulation by the more powerful banking interests, as the RFC case illustrated so nicely. By 1933 the stage was set for a change in bank regulation and the introduction of a government-centered solution.

Even before the conclusion of the Pecora hearings, events that foreshadowed the end of financial-industry dominance of the policy process were unfolding at a rapid pace. In allowing weak banks to fail, the financial-industry solution encouraged a run on solvent institutions, further worsening the crisis. State authorities responded with local moratoria, or bank holidays, to stem runs. These bank holidays simply closed banks via state proclamation in the hope of preventing panicked depositors from withdrawing their funds and causing the failure of otherwise sound banks. By early 1933, moratoria had been declared in twenty-one states, with the remainder in dire straits (Burns 1974, 27; Kennedy 1973, 146–147). The problem with the state bank holidays was that they left national banks exposed to panicked depositors.

With congressional consent, and after consultation with member banks, the New York and Chicago Federal Reserve Banks called for a bank holiday in their districts. The Federal Reserve Board extended the call to all those states in which banks were still open. Upon his inauguration, President Roosevelt set his cabinet to work on draft legislation that declared a bank holiday. This bought the necessary time for Congress to consider emergency banking legislation drafted by the White House.

The Emergency Banking Act, issued at the end of the "holiday," was primarily the work of the New York Federal Reserve Bank. It provided a mechanism for reopening all sound banks, reorganizing salvageable institutions, and liquidating hopeless cases. The Federal Reserve Banks were given the primary role in implementing the act. The act served notice to the financial industry that they had lost the prerogative in formulating a solution to the banking crisis.

Public, press, and congressional support for bank reform was at an all-time high at the close of the Pecora hearings and the end of the bank holiday. Carter Glass introduced a bill on March 11 that looked much like the old Glass bill. Senator Thomas P. Gore offered a joint resolution of his own, calling for an amendment that would give Congress control of all banking in the United States. The Federal Reserve provided the Senate Banking Committee with a draft proposal creating a single national banking system for all commercial banks. The message was clear to the shattered banking coalition: The provisions of the Glass bill appeared mild compared to some reform suggestions coming out of Congress.

Constructing the New Deal System: The Banking Act of 1933

In mid-March 1933, the White House held a conference to consider banking legislation. All the major public actors from the financial subsystem were in attendance. The secretary of the Treasury, members of the Federal Reserve Board, Senator Glass, and the chairs of the House and Senate Banking Committees—Henry B. Steagall and Duncan Fletcher, respectively—settled on the Glass bill as the vehicle to guide reform. Leading the way, the administration announced its intention of establishing "a permanently united and coherent banking system through the Federal Reserve system" (Burns 1974, 80). With this is mind, Glass and Steagall each introduced revised banking bills in the Senate and House in May. The bills separated commercial banking from investment banking, granted branching rights to national banks in states that allowed state-chartered institutions that privilege, increased capital requirements for national banks, established a temporary deposit-insurance fund, and subjected holding-company operations involving national banks to OCC regulation.[10] Like the earlier Glass proposal, each of the provisions in the Banking Act of 1933 was the subject of a good deal of scrutiny within the financial subsystem.

The provision subject to the least debate was the portion of the act separating investment from commercial banking. The Pecora hearings were the catalyst that ended the ability of the banking community to block attempts to enforce the separation of investment from commercial banking. Glass had been pushing for active enforcement of separation, which actually existed in law before 1933. The stock market abuses and just plain ineptitude exhibited by so many banks made the separation hard to argue against. Many of the large money-center banks in New York, most notably Chase National Bank and J. P. Morgan and Company, read the writing on the wall and "voluntarily" began to separate their investment activity from commercial banking before the passage of the act; the rest of the industry was quick to follow suit (Kennedy 1973, 212–213). The separation of commercial and investment banking was an important first step toward creating a new, more narrowly focused financial subsystem. It established the parameters of the New Deal regulatory system through the institutionalization of separation-by-function criteria and an emphasis on creating sound financial institutions through prudent regulation.

Branching, however, went nowhere. This was clear evidence of the staying power of the original core belief dealing with the concentration of economic power. Still, inroads were made by those favoring increased regulatory control over individual bank management. The reform bill allowed the comptroller or Federal Reserve to remove the officers or directors of any national bank or member of the Federal Reserve system that continued to violate safety regulations after federal notification. As was the case with the new capitalization requirements, state banks were not affected by the preceding unless they sought membership in the Federal Reserve or deposit insurance. In both cases the financial industry was able to secure exceptions that allowed banks an "out" if regulations proved too onerous.

The topic of deposit insurance split the financial subsystem and political system like no other provision of the banking reform. Within the subsystem the issue pitted pro-insurance forces (mostly small unit banks), led by Steagall, against regulators, Senator Glass, and the remainder of the financial industry. A similar split existed within the administration—President Roosevelt threatened to veto any bill containing an insurance provision, and former Speaker of the House and current vice-president, John Nance Garner, was an advocate of deposit insurance. The pro-insurance forces were joined by several prominent Democrats, most notably California's Senator William Gibbs McAdoo, from the Banking Committee; the American Federation of Labor; and a large slice of public opinion. Glass offered a compromise that made insurance a temporary phenomenon under a "sinking fund" provision, although full insurance was still an integral part of the House plan. In the end a compromise on the Glass compromise was accepted, making insurance temporary but dropping the provisions in the Glass plan that also made insurance self-liquidating.

The Banking Act of 1933 was reported out of conference on June 13. Both chambers accepted the conference report, and the president signed the bill into law on June 16. The act represented a series of compromises among key subsystem players, mediated by the role of several nonsubsystem actors or forces. State member banks, aided by non–Banking Committee legislators, successfully fought the attempt to create a single national system and greatly modified original branching proposals. They were joined in the latter effort by nationally chartered small banks, which personified the split in the banking industry (and the banking subsystem). Deposit insurance was the product of compromise between unit banks and larger institutions and between the House and Senate Banking Committees.[11] Once again a deciding factor was a variable external to the subsystem; in this case public opinion did the trick. Similarly, the separation of investment and deposit banking, agreed to by key subsystem players, was aided by the salience-raising efforts of Senate hearings.

The passage of the Banking Act of 1933 was made possible in part by the near collapse of the economy and the disarray in the financial industry in particular.

The sorry state of banking convinced a large segment of bankers, regulators, politicians, and the public that something needed to be done. The principles enshrined in the 1933 legislation represented a shift away from the belief that banking was simply another business endeavor to be governed by the principles of the market (see Table 2.3). The change in beliefs was itself a long time coming. The "system" debate had its roots in the turn-of-the-century discussions leading up to the adoption of the Federal Reserve Act. The 1933 act was the culmination of the ongoing discussion, settled in favor of those who insisted banking was different and should be subjected to regulation.

In the early years of the Federal Reserve, there were both recognition that banks coexisted in a system and a set of limits on government players charged with enforcing system rules. That is, the business of banking was conducted with only loose guidance from regulators. The Fed served as an emergency system of coordination for member banks, coming to life during crisis until the danger of panic passed (Kennedy 1973, 8–9). Thus although banks recognized they were part of a system, they still preferred to act as independent agents in most instances. This individualistic ethos proved disastrous during the depression.

The 1933 act settled on safety and soundness as key principles of bank regulation. It created a system intent on protecting depositors from bank malfeasance as well as on saving banks from themselves. New Deal regulation produced specialized financial intermediaries, each serving a distinct set of customers, each with its own market share carved out vis-à-vis regulation. The design of the regulation was intended to foster the growth of the system ideal. The passage of de-

TABLE 2.3 The New Deal Regulatory System, 1933–1980

Policy Core Beliefs	*Programmatic Incarnations*
Normative	
1. Industry must be preserved.	1. Regulation Q
2. Consumers must be protected.	2. Limited interstate banking
3. Concentration of power is bad.	3. No branching
4. Markets are destructive.	4. Investment restrictions
5. Regulation is a matter of management.	5. Consumers protected via regulatory prohibitions
6. Banking is distinct from other forms of business.	6. Deposit insurance
Empirical	7. Charter granting
1. Emphasize regulation; allow controlled competition.	8. Examinations
2. Dual regulation should be divided between national and state authorities.	
3. Regulation is divided among OCC, Fed, FDIC, and FHLBB.	
4. Financial intermediaries are separated according to function.	

posit insurance both protected consumers in a fashion unique to banking and compelled the management of large banks to keep an eye on small institutions so as to avoid the costs of a bailout through insurance. Regulators were given both policing and managerial goals in the new regulatory setup. Not only were banks to be kept on a tight regulatory leash when it came to investments (policing), they were also to be managed via regulation so as to better serve clientele in their particular share of the market. As the preceding section indicated, many banks did not come to the system table willingly. New Deal regulation was like bailing out a drowning man who wasn't entirely convinced he was drowning. The office of the president was used to compel banks to join a system that was itself still in flux. Nowhere is this more apparent than in the events leading up to the passage of the Banking Act of 1935.

Putting the Fed into the Federal Reserve System: The Banking Act of 1935

The Banking Act of 1935 represented an attempt by banks to win back some of the things they had lost with the passage of the 1933 legislation. It contained three sections: Title I dealt with the liberalization of the rate and nature of FDIC assessment; Title II contained proposed changes in the Federal Reserve system; and Title III granted relief to bank officers required by the 1933 act to liquidate their loans by July 1, 1935. The first and third sections were generally supported by and favorable to the banking community. Indeed, they were responses to the intense lobbying campaign that had accompanied attempts to implement the 1933 act. The second section of the 1935 act enshrined the goals of the newly appointed governor of the Federal Reserve Board, Marriner Eccles. Eccles sought to establish once and for all the preeminent power of the Fed Board in the banking system. Title II engendered no shortage of financial-industry and regulator protest when it was introduced. The passage of the 1935 Bank Act is important because it institutionalized the power of the Fed Board in the banking system. On the flip side, it also eased the president out of the business of bank regulation, moving subsystem politics back toward a bank-dominant equilibrium.

Marriner Eccles accepted appointment to the Federal Reserve Board with the understanding that he would be allowed to refashion the role of the board in the system. Eccles was intent on creating a board able to accomplish two interrelated goals: control of the money supply and promotion of business stability. Centralizing power in the board put the Fed in direct opposition to a sizable portion of the coalition that had produced the Bank Act of 1933, most notably Carter Glass, the Federal Reserve branch banks, and the majority of the banking fraternity. Eccles began restructuring the board–branch bank relationship even before legislation was submitted to Congress. Upon assuming the governorship of the board he dissolved the branch bank–dominated System Committee on Legislation, substituting a new committee composed of board members. It was this committee that did much of the work on the 1935 banking legislation (Burns 1974, 142–144).

The Fed changes were essential to the recovery program of the New Deal, which called for large-scale government spending that in turn required financing by a joint public-private effort coordinated by the Federal Reserve. Roosevelt did not trust the banking industry–controlled branch banks with a veto over his recovery program, having witnessed the failure of previous branch bank efforts to restart the economy under the NCC and RFC. The 1935 banking bill spent a rocky few months in the Senate due to hurt feelings on the part of Senator Glass, who had been bypassed by the White House and who responded by stonewalling the bill; the legislation was reported out of Congress as the Bank Act of 1935.

The act reduced the Fed Board of Governors to seven members appointed by the president and serving staggered fourteen-year terms. The Treasury and OCC positions were removed from the board. Reserve bank presidents served five-year terms and were appointed by the boards of directors of the individual Reserve banks subject to the approval of the board of governors. The act created the Open Market Committee (OMC), consisting of the members of the board and five representatives of the Reserve banks selected annually and charged with buying and selling government securities.[12] The board was also granted increased powers over setting reserve requirements—the amount of money banks must hold in reserve against deposits. The definition of eligible paper—the type of assets banks could count as part of reserves—was broadened, and restrictions on real estate loans by national banks were eased. These latter two provisions were meant to lessen the objections by banks to the increased regulatory authority of the Federal Reserve Board. Titles I and III were enacted with little change, providing the financial industry the relief it sought from portions of the 1933 Bank Act.

The New Deal Reforms: A Brief Summary

The initial response to the banking crisis that accompanied the Great Depression was to treat it as a matter suitable for a purely private solution. President Hoover, in choosing to define the problem as a private matter, abdicated any significant role for the White House in formulating a response to the banking crisis. Hoover accepted the argument by banks that the financial subsystem could deal with the problem, that it was a matter best left to insiders. Several private, or quasi-public but privately managed, solutions were experimented with by the industry-led coalition. All such attempts were found wanting by a significant segment of actors within and external to the financial subsystem. The lack of success by the financial-industry coalition led to a reassessment of the belief that market-like solutions or temporary, quasi-public expedients would solve the problems facing the financial industry. The 1933 act was recognition of the failings of financial industry–led attempts.

Title II of the 1935 act was introduced because it was essential to the realization of President Roosevelt's plans for economic recovery, plans that required the cooperation of the financial industry and better coordination of monetary policy. Title II granted the Federal Reserve Board broad powers over the money supply, in addition to a host of regulatory responsibilities added by Fed chair Marriner Eccles during hearings. A principal goal of Title II was ensuring that the New Deal would not be left hostage to the whims of the financial industry. In this fashion Title II created a regulatory actor, in the form of a newly empowered Federal Reserve Board, that enjoyed a degree of independence from both the financial industry and other institutional players. Presidential intervention was instrumental to secure the passage of the act. Ironically, much of the increased regulatory authority granted the Fed was an unintended consequence of the presidential pursuit of economic recovery. In the case of Title II, the Federal Reserve used presidential concerns with economic recovery to establish its place in the financial subsystem.

EXPLAINING CHANGING POLITICS IN THE FINANCIAL SUBSYSTEM

The development of the Federal Reserve System and its current incarnation as the bedrock of New Deal regulation illustrate several key features of subsystem development as well as highlight the dynamic of subsystem politics.

Subsystem Development

Subsystems are, in the words of Frank Baumgartner and Bryan Jones (1993), policy monopolies sustained by an identifiable set of ideas and institutional arrangements. Quite simply, they are arrangements by which select players decide the course of public policy. One is struck by the predominance of financial regulators, banking experts, and the financial industry in the various efforts at idea definition and institution building that produced the Federal Reserve system—and the financial subsystem.

Many of the finer points of banking are beyond the understanding of the uninitiated. Arguments about currency inelasticity, the meaning of "money," what drives interest rates up or down, and the like involve a realm of knowledge familiar to very few. The degree of complexity plays into the major goal of subsystem actors first enunciated by the National Monetary Commission: to keep "politics" out of discussions of financial regulation. This involves limiting participation in the policy process to a select few intimately associated with the business of banking. Expertise and material self-interest are common bonds that serve this limiting function and hold the subsystem together.

Much of the activity that determines the shape of the financial subsystem has a congressional locus. The banking committees are a key stop-off in attempts to promote or prevent regulatory change, with committee or subcommittee chairs playing a significant role in the process. Regulators are often instrumental in defining problems and offering solutions. From the early attempts to fashion a central bank, in which the OCC and Treasury figured prominently, to the strengthening of the Federal Reserve Board orchestrated by Marriner Eccles, regulators have played an essential role as architects of the regulatory system. To argue that these "regulars" dominate is not to suggest that they always act in concert or unfettered but simply that bank-dominant coalitions are the norm in the financial subsystem.

During the formation of the Federal Reserve system, for example, outsiders were important in shaping the debate. In the initial reform discussion, consumers of credit—corporate capital and farmers—were prime shapers of ideas. During the New Deal, business interests were again important, as were depositors who sought protection via regulation. In both instances outsiders were able to exercise influence when events in the larger system proved too much for subsystem arrangements to handle, which brings us to the topic of change or variation in subsystem politics.

The Dynamic of Subsystem Politics

The story of the development and evolution of the Federal Reserve system, and in effect the financial subsystem, illustrates the dynamic of subsystem change. Subsystem insiders attempt to effect closure with regard to participation in policy-making, that is, to maintain bank-coalition dominance. Their ability to do so, however, is determined by the mix of challenges—institutional, party-based, and economic—to subsystem arrangements.

As was suggested in Chapter 1, institutional conflict is a key determinant of subsystem politics and the type of policy produced in the subsystem setting. As the preceding case study demonstrates, the president made his presence felt in the design of financial regulation. In the role of agenda setter, the White House provided the necessary muscle to get the system-oriented solution onto the decision agenda. Presidential involvement was a key variable in the passage and design of the Federal Reserve Act, as well as the Bank Acts of 1933 and 1935. Still, presidential coalitions are transitory phenomena. Experts move on to new issues or their advice goes out of fashion, presidential attention invariably wanders abroad, and stray legislators fade from sight when their objectives are met or they tire of the subsystem game.

Party politics also played an important part in the formation and evolution of the financial subsystem. The systems ideal was originally enunciated by Charles Fowler, a Republican, but Democrats were the major architects of the financial subsystem in the twentieth century. Indeed, it was the split among Republicans that allowed Woodrow Wilson to assume the presidency and Democrats to gain control of Congress. Once in control they created a Federal Reserve that would serve as an important institutional element of the financial subsystem. It was the shift in party control during the Great Depression, again from Republican to Democrat, that sparked redesign of the Federal Reserve and financial regulation.

Party politics were not only important in opening the door for presidential involvement, they also provided the catalyst for congressionally authored change.

Economic dislocation has been an almost constant shaper of subsystem politics and policy outputs. It was the series of recessions and depressions at the turn of the century that convinced banks, business, regulators, and politicians that some type of regulatory system was a necessity. The Great Depression was the force behind the perfection of the New Deal regulatory system and the catalyst that eventually reunited the banking industry. The creation of a "panic proof" system was nothing more than an attempt to insulate banking from the vagaries of the business cycle and outsider interference in the business of banking.

Finally, and not unexpectedly, the regulated industry is a key player in the policy process. And as the New Deal and Federal Reserve case studies illustrate, the financial industry is not necessarily united on all issues. In the case of the initial New Deal legislation, it was the split between large and small banks into opposing coalitions during 1933 that, when combined with events in the larger environment, allowed reformers to get a foot in the door and rewrite financial regulation. Yet the events surrounding the 1935 Bank Act also demonstrate how short lived such financial-industry splits are. In the case of Titles I and III of the 1935 act, the regulated clearly came together when outside interests threatened to upset fundamental subsystem arrangements. Indeed, New Deal regulation created a truce of sorts between the various banking factions. After 1935 it was clear to the members of the banking fraternity that unity was essential if they were to keep the financial subsystem alive. Thus the events of the 1930s were the final act in the creation of the financial subsystem. New Deal regulation created a set of institutions and rules that fostered cooperation and unity among disparate financial institutions through the 1980s.

In the remaining chapters I am concerned with detailing how the wavering equilibrium that is the financial subsystem functions over a longer period of time. In order to do this, in Chapter 3, I develop a more fully refined indicator of subsystem political variation and use it to map political change over a seventy-year time span.

3

Who Is on First? Mapping
Subsystem Political Change

Chapter 1 wound its way through the thicket of subsystems literature, suggesting that the various permutations could be placed on a subsystem continuum containing three variations. Chapter 2 traced the birth and evolution of the financial subsystem, illustrating both the dynamic of change and its effect on policy outcomes. This chapter lays the groundwork for extending our inquiry to a longer time frame by mapping variation in the financial subsystem over a seventy-year time span, from 1919 through 1988. It does so through the development and application of a congressionally based measure of subsystem politics that focuses on the identity of participants at hearings.

RESEARCH DESIGN

I use an adaptation of Keith Hamm's (1986) approach to map political variation in the financial subsystem over time and across particular policy areas.[1] Variation in subsystem politics is mapped through a congressionally based measure that takes note of the identity of interests intimately involved in the formulation of financial regulation. In addition, care is taken to note the concentration of "interesteds" on the banking committees for each session of Congress and the relationship between interesteds and subsystem politics.

Interesteds

Subsystem theory recognizes that congressional committees are the key institutional building block of policy monopolies. Thus it is often assumed that committees are filled with "preference outliers" or "interesteds." Interested committee members are distinguished from their legislative peers by occupational or group membership held in common with the interests the committee regulates, serves, or oversees. There are a number of studies that examine the impact of shared interests on the policy process. Some find that the presence of interesteds on a committee has an impact on policy outcomes in a seemingly direct fashion (Maass

1951; Jones 1961; Freeman 1965; Shepsle 1978; Hamm 1986); others suggest the impact is conditioned by intervening variables (Oppenheimer 1974) or insignificant (Bond 1979). An interested is defined as any committee member who has a background in or connection to the financial industry. The *Biographical Directory of the American Congress* was consulted to determine the occupational background of committee members. Any member who listed his or her occupation as banker or thrift officer or was connected to any type of financial institution was classified as an interested.

Participation Profiles

At the heart of subsystems theory is the notion that policymaking responsibilities have devolved to select actors. A major task confronting anyone interested in policymaking by subsystem involves documenting the identity of these key players. This study settles on a hearing-based indicator of subsystem political variation. The choice of such a measure is intimately connected to the actual function hearings serve in the policy process. Charles Jones (1982, 352) argues that Congress serves as the political system's "principal legitimizer" and as such "is a stage on which one may witness all the principal actors participating in issue-related dramas." More recent observers suggest that congressional committees "are mechanisms for devolving policymaking to subsystems" (Jones, Baumgartner, and Talbert 1993, 657). If Congress is the stage and committees the medium, a major act in the policy drama is the congressional hearing. Hearings serve as a forum in which the various participants in the subsystem come together to bargain over proposed alterations in the resource configuration in the subsystem. Hearings serve as a conduit for information and communications between subsystem participants, a court of sorts where facts are established, and a setting in which proposals for change are marketed. Hearings involve key players in everything from problem recognition to agenda setting, formulation, and legitimation (Baumgartner and Jones 1993; Jones, Baumgartner, and Talbert 1993; Talbert, Baumgartner, and Jones 1995; Leyden 1995). I suggest hearings serve as a barometer of the political climate, faithfully registering any change in interest group pressure in the subsystem.

In order to delimit subsystem politics for a particular session of Congress, witness-concentration ratios characteristic of the three subsystem variants discussed in Chapter 1 were constructed as follows (see the methodological appendix at the end of this chapter for a more detailed discussion of the construction of the participation profiles). If the ratio of bank regulators and banks to total witnesses equaled or surpassed the mean figure for the seventy-year time period and the figure for outsiders (see further on) did not equal the seventy-year mean, that particular congress was classified as typical of *dominant coalition* politics. There are several substantive and theoretical reasons to expect hearings in which the regulated and regulators dominate to produce outcomes that favor the regulated.

Chapter 2 demonstrated how the financial industry serves as a key clearance point for any proposed changes to the institutional outlines of financial regulation. When financial-industry interests dominate hearings, it is no surprise they play a large role in shaping policy. The notion of dominant coalitions suggests that banking interests have an inside track in determining the shape of financial regulation. It also suggests that such politics are the norm in the financial subsystem.

The ratio of nonbanking interest groups, nonbank regulators, and state politicos and regulators to total witnesses serves as an indicator of politics characteristic of *competitive coalitions*. If the figure for these three interests equaled or surpassed the seventy-year mean and the figure for banking interests did not equal its mean, the congress was classified as typical of competitive coalitions.

These three collections of actors were chosen because they represent the most potent rivals to financial industry and national regulatory hegemony in the financial subsystem. State-chartered banks are the natural rival of national banks in the dual-banking system. Non-financial-industry interest groups consist of three sets of interests. The first are the "nonbank banks"—the securities industry, retailers such as Sears, credit card companies along the lines of American Express, the insurance industry, and the like—all of which are represented by well-established trade associations. Consumer groups and retailer associations are the other two predominant outsiders. Each of the factions among this collection of actors is represented by well-funded, long-established interest groups. In addition to their interest group base, each is accompanied by federal and/ or state regulatory authorities from other subsystems, further serving to divide consensus within the subsystem.

If a session of Congress failed to meet the criteria of either of the preceding, it was classified as typical of *transitory coalitions*. Typically, such a session was marked by the participation of a mixed bag of outsiders including White House personnel, academics, and stray non–Banking Committee legislators. The presence of this disparate collection of actors indicates that the subsystem is more permeable than the dominant scenario would have it but is not subject to as concerted an assault as envisioned by the competitive scenario.

Mapping the politics of the financial subsystem via a legislature-based measure presents one with an interesting dilemma: Most subsystem studies ignore the bicameral nature of Congress when developing a model of subsystem relations. They assume that the House and Senate, as legislative institutions, do not present significantly different institutional contexts for subsystem players. Whereas this might be a valid assumption when one compares legislatures to other institutional or organizational settings, the proposition that the House and Senate are so alike as to be indistinguishable is a hypothesis for testing rather than an accepted fact. Indeed, there is a sizable body of literature that makes one uncomfortable with such a suggestion (Matthews 1960; Fenno 1973; Jones 1982; Davidson 1989; Longley and Oleszek 1989; Smith and Deering 1990). So that the similarities and differences between chambers may be better understood, this chapter treats each separately.

MAPPING THE FINANCIAL SUBSYSTEM

We begin the process of mapping the financial subsystem with an examination of the presence of interesteds on each of the banking committees between 1919 and 1988. This is followed by an exercise that develops a seventy-year panorama of the politics of financial regulation.

Interesteds on the House and
Senate Banking Committees

One might suggest that if banks are interested in maintaining a policy monopoly in the area of financial regulation, they set their sights on the membership of the banking committees. Table 3.1 and Figure 3.1 document the wide variation in the fraction of interesteds on the House and Senate Banking Committees through time. Overrepresentation was determined by comparing the fraction of interesteds on the committee with the percentage of legislators with banking experience in the chamber as a whole. If the fraction on the committee is larger than the fraction for the chamber, interesteds are overrepresented on the committee.

As the table indicates, thirty of thirty-five sessions had an overrepresentation of interesteds on one of the banking committees. Of these thirty sessions, twenty-five meet the requisites of overrepresentation in both the House and Senate (1920–1953, 1955–1963, and 1982–1988). Nine of the preceding also have a chair who is an interested. At the very least, these seven sessions represent periods in which industry interests would appear to have a leg up on other interests. That is, they are sessions in which a sizable portion of majority members on the committee, including the chair, are themselves bankers or otherwise intimately tied to the financial industry.

It is no surprise that most of the sessions are characterized by an overrepresentation of interesteds on the committee. Legislators with a background in the financial industry appear to act like legislators with other types of substantive interests: They flock to the committee that deals with that interest. Still, there is some variation in the degree to which interesteds are overrepresented. That is, at times the fraction of members with a background in the financial industry is quite close to that of the chamber as a whole; at others it dwarfs the figure for the chamber.

In both the Senate and House the fraction of interesteds on the committee declines over time, roughly paralleling the expansion of interests involved in hearings (as the following section demonstrates) as well as the increasingly diverse policy tasks entrusted to the committee. The fraction of interesteds on the committees manifests a strong negative trend over time; this decrease is arrested in the late 1970s, when a weak positive trend develops.

Now let us move on to an examination of the mix of witnesses at hearings. The following section opens with an examination of the House, moves on to the Senate, and concludes with a comparison of the two.

TABLE 3.1   Interesteds on the House and Senate Banking Committees (percentages)

Year	House	Senate
1920	40c	31
1922	38c	33
1924	29c	20
1926	29c	20
1928	24c	13
1930	29c	44
1932	33	37
1934	20	35
1936	20	26
1938	20	26
1940	24	30
1942	24	30
1944	23	25
1946	30	32
1948	26	31c
1950	15	31
1952	22	23
1954	10	33
1956	14	33c
1958	14	20c
1960	20	20
1962	24	13
1964	18	0
1966	9	0
1968	6	0
1970	6	0
1972	2	0
1974	5	0
1976	5c	8
1978	6c	0
1980	7c	6
1982	9	6
1984	9	11
1986	8	13
1988	8	11

Note: Bold indicates that interesteds are overrepresented; "c" indicates that the chair is an interested.

Mapping Subsystem Political Change

Figure 3.2 maps variation in subsystem politics from 1919 to 1920, the 66th Congress, through 1987–1988, the 100th Congress, for the House, Senate, and Congress as a whole (for a more detailed treatment of participation in the House, see Table 3.2 in the appendix to this chapter). Four rather distinct periods of politics

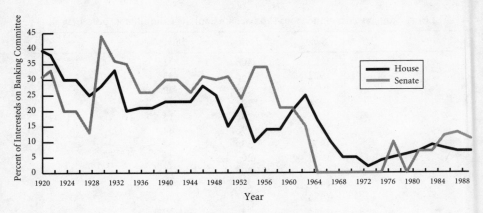

FIGURE 3.1   Interesteds on the House and Senate Banking Committees

in the House stand out. The first, typical of competitive coalitions, runs from 1933 through 1938. This period corresponds with the New Deal banking reforms discussed in Chapter 2. The second period runs from 1939 through 1948 and is dominated by a financial industry intent on reasserting control over financial regulation. A third phase of dominant politics begins again in 1953 and runs pretty much unabated through 1968. The final period, 1969 through 1988, is marked by the politics of competing coalitions. This last phase corresponds with the rise of the consumer movement, the entry of nonbank banks into the realm of financial services, and the partial deregulation of banking (the subject of Chapter 7).

Three extended periods of politics stand out in the Senate. The first, from 1927 through 1940, corresponds with competing coalitions and occurs during the New Deal banking reforms discussed in Chapter 2. A second period, beginning in 1941 and running through 1960, is typical of dominant coalitions. A final period, beginning in 1975 and running through 1998, is typical of competitive coalitions and corresponds with the rise of deregulation and internal disruptions within the financial subsystem.

Congress	T T B T C T T C C C T B B B B T B B B B B T C B T C T T C C T C C C C
Senate	C C B B C C T C C C C B B B B B B B B B B C C B C C B T C C B C C C C
House	B B B C C B B C C C B B B B B C B B B B B B C B B C C B C C C C C C C

1920   1940   1960   1980

B = Bank-dominant coalition
C = Competitive coalitions
T = Transitory coalitions

FIGURE 3.2   Political variation in the financial subsystem, 1920 to 1987–1988

Combining the chamber-based political indicators produces a Congress-based portrait of financial subsystem politics that contains four identifiable political phases. The first, 1919 through 1926, involves transitory coalitions involved in a debate over the role and purpose of the Federal Reserve system (detailed in Chapter 2). This first phase is unusual in that transitory coalitions are normally a temporary phenomenon. The eight-year hiatus can be explained by the relatively tender age of the financial subsystem. As detailed in Chapter 2, the creation of the Federal Reserve was in fact the birth of the financial subsystem. The actual maturation of the subsystem was stalled by World War I and the following struggle over the locus of control (see Chapter 2).

A second phase of competitive coalitions kicks in following the stock market crash and the ensuing economic depression, 1928 through 1938. During this phase the New Deal banking reforms settle the question of Federal Reserve control, clearly demarcate the business of banking from other forms of economic endeavor, and institutionalize the parameters of the financial subsystem. This is followed by a brief period of transitory coalitions, 1939–1940, that serves to usher in a twenty-year run of dominant coalitions, 1941–1960.

The period of bank dominance coincides with the onset of World War II, the rebirth of the U.S. economy, and the postwar boom of the 1950s. The war, and the rebuilding process following the cessation of hostilities, served to fuel an economic boom during which banks prospered. It also marked the entrance of banks into new fields of business (as detailed in Chapter 6) and relative quiet on the regulatory front.

Following the twenty-year reign of the banks, a chaos of sorts sets in. Politics jumps from one variation to another with no lasting trend until the mid-1970s. This is a period marked by economic turmoil—beginning with a slowdown in housing starts and a decline in economic growth in the early 1960s and ending with the stagflation of the 1970s. The final phase, 1975 through 1988, is characterized by competing coalitions. Ushered in by two studies critical of banking practices and regulation (the subject of Chapter 7), pushed along by technological changes, fueled by the consumer movement and rival "nonbank banks," this phase ends with an attempt to deregulate the financial industry.

All the preceding portraits of interest politics—House, Senate, and Congress—highlight an interesting feature of the financial subsystem. Politics go through a cycle of sorts, varying between permeable and nonpermeable, with an overall trend of increased permeability over time. Indeed, the last period of competitive coalitions corresponds with the general trend of increased public interest group involvement in politics noted by a number of observers (Moe 1981; Gais, Peterson, and Walker 1984; Wilson 1981; Eisner 1993).

A permeable and less permeable dynamic also occurs during the periods of mixed politics—that is, those periods in which House- and Senate-based politics do not mirror one another. Subsystem politics shifts from competitive to dominant as one crosses between the two institutional poles (House and Senate), so that in the interim periods interest groups can, and do, engage in forum shopping. As suggested earlier, subsystems are a wavering-equilibrium solution to the policy puzzle. That is, their resilience has a good deal to do with their flexibility, flexibility that allows interest groups frozen out in one institutional forum—the House or Senate—to make their case in the other. Flexibility also means that when faced with environmental or system-level changes or challenges, the subsystem moves to accommodate challengers while maintaining institutional integrity. That is, politics varies as a response to changing times. Most notable among the stimuli are economic changes—ranging from recession to depression, political stimulus in the form of a change in presidential administration, and change in the general shape of the interest group universe (for a more detailed treatment of the preceding factors see Chapters 2, 6, and 7).

It is important to note the fleeting nature of the transitory scenario. It does not occur very often, never in the House and only twice in the Senate. It appears, then, that subsystem dynamics gravitate toward an interest group–based equilibrium. This finding is not at all surprising; subsystems are founded and maintained by well-organized groups of interests. Because this is so, Thurber (1991) suggests that subsystem-based equilibriums tend toward dominant politics. Indeed, a rationale for establishing subsystems is to avoid the competition and anarchy of the larger political system. Still, the preceding suggests that competition is a real possibility (for a similar line of argument see Johnson 1992). The point is that competition is controlled vis-à-vis channeling through the institutional bedrock of subsystems, the congressional committee system. What may surprise some adherents of the subsystem framework is that outsiders can and do play an important role in subsystem policy discourse.

Although the match is not perfect across the House- and Senate-based subsystems, the periods of rough correspondence between politics in the House and Senate indicate a strong connection between the two. Both are marked by a similar cycle. Still, there are large enough gaps during select periods to discourage one from abandoning the notion of dual subsystems completely. Having tracked subsystem political variation over time, I move to a brief consideration of one of the engines of political change—the salience of banking policy.

ISSUE SALIENCE, MEDIA ATTENTION, AND SUBSYSTEM POLITICS

Frank Baumgartner and Bryan Jones (1993, 59) suggest that media coverage is linked to political elite and public attention to any given issue. Increased attention brings the day-to-day operations of subsystems under intense scrutiny and is thus to be avoided at all costs. In the eyes of subsystem regulars, no news is good news. This is because as attention increases, acceptance declines (Baumgartner and Jones 1993, 64). As with the making of sausage, the more folks know about subsystem business, the less likely they are to support it.

In order to get a feel for the changing salience of banking policy, story counts were tabulated using the *Reader's Guide to Periodical Literature* (see the chapter appendix for a more detailed discussion of coding). All told, 4,962 stories dealing with banking appeared in the *Reader's Guide* between 1919 and 1988. Given the two-year time frame of Congress, story counts were combined into two-year segments to aid in analysis (see Figure 3.3). Media attention to banking varies dramatically over time, from a low of 40 stories in 1919–1920 to a high of 400 in 1983–1984, averaging 142 stories per two-year segment. The periods of highest salience coincide with two of the more tumultuous periods in financial regulation. The first, 1929 through 1936, includes the Great Depression and the New Deal banking reforms discussed in Chapter 2. The second period, beginning in 1976 and running through 1988, is the era of consumer protection, the nonbank banks, and deregulation (to be discussed in Chapter 7).

The relationship between salience and subsystem politics is much as one would expect. Fewer banking stories appear in the media during periods of dominant politics (86 stories on average in the House and 89 in the Senate) than is the case in competitive coalitions (211 and 183 stories, respectively). If the tone of coverage is controlled for, the ratio of positive to negative stories shows remarkable consistency across chambers. Under the dominant scenario, it is 1.24 in the House and 1.26 in the Senate; under competitive politics the figures are .37 and .39, respectively. Clearly, heightened salience is associated with more open politics and more critical coverage of banking affairs. Thus "increased news is usually bad news" for subsystem insiders in that it opens policymaking to increased outsider participation and conflict.

SUMMARY AND CONCLUSION

The primary task of this chapter is exploratory: to develop a more systematic means of documenting change in subsystem politics over a longer time frame than case studies allow. The chapter develops a multilayered portrait of subsystem

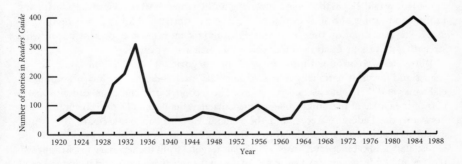

FIGURE 3.3   The changing salience of banking policy, 1919–1988

politics, suggesting the system consists of two semidistinct subsystems centered around the House and Senate (for a similar line of argument about subsystems in general, see Huitt 1968). Variation in subsystem politics appears to be associated with changes in the salience of banking as an issue on the public agenda, as well as with systemic events—the Great Depression, the post–World War II economic boom, and deregulation in the 1980s. I explore the dynamic of subsystem politics in greater detail in Chapters 6 and 7.

What is the effect of changes in salience, interest group participation, and the like on the course of financial regulation? Do outsider coalitions really result in effective participation by non-subsystem regulars in the policy process? If so, what is the result of such participation? In Chapter 4, I consider these questions and more, focusing on the effect of subsystem political change on the mechanics of the legislative process through an examination of agenda setting and policy formulation.

APPENDIX

Constructing Participation Profiles

Witness-concentration ratios were constructed as follows. Using the U.S. Congress *Index of Congressional Committee Hearings*, all House and Senate Banking Committee hearings were reviewed on a session-by-session basis so as to identify those dealing with domestic financial regulation. A second search was conducted using the *Congressional Record Index*. A final search was conducted using the Congressional Information Service's *U.S. Congress Committee Hearing Index*. These latter searches were necessary in order to include hearings that occurred outside the banking committees' venue and also served as a double check of the original search process. The indices are subject matter–based. Keywords used in the search include bank failure, banks and banking, commercial banks, Federal Deposit Insurance Corporation, Federal Home Loan Bank Board, Federal Reserve banks, Federal Reserve Board, Federal Reserve system, savings and loans, thrifts, and a variety of subject-specific headings such as NOW accounts, electronic fund transfers, and the like.

Lists of witnesses were gathered from the abstracts of the hearings in the Congressional Information Service's *U.S. Congress Committee Hearing Index*. All told, 448 hearings, 225 in the House and 223 in the Senate, involving 5,799 witnesses were reviewed. Participation profiles, indicating who shows up at hearings, were constructed for each session of Congress. The participation profiles indicate not only if an interest is present but in what strength—that is, the fraction of witnesses of a particular type.

Witnesses were grouped into one of eight categories. The first, banks, includes all shapes and forms of nationally chartered financial intermediaries—principally commercial banks and thrifts but also credit unions. The second, bank regulators, contains members of the Office of the Comptroller of the Currency, the Federal Deposit Insurance Corporation, the Federal Reserve, and the Federal Home Loan Bank Board. The third, executive-branch actors, includes anyone from the executive office of the president, White House staff, and cabinet-level Treasury officials ranging from the secretary to assistant secretaries and undersecretaries. Legislators make up the fourth category and include all non-banking committee members of Congress. Academics, the fifth category, includes a range of policy intellectuals from university faculty to members of think tanks such as Brookings and the American Enterprise Institution. The sixth, other regulators, contains a variety of federal regulators—from members of the Securities and Exchange Commission to lawyers from the Justice Department. State-level regulators, the seventh category, is principally made up of state-level financial regulators and assorted state-level elected officials. The eighth, rival interests, consists of securities firms, insurance companies, credit card companies, and public interest and consumer groups. Tables 3.2 and 3.3 contain the results of the coding exercise.

Issue Salience and Media Attention

Borrowing from Baumgartner and Jones (1993), I used entries in the *Readers' Guide to Periodical Literature* as an indicator of salience on the public agenda. I was interested in gathering two kinds of data—the sheer number of stories and the tone of coverage. The first was relatively simple to do once keywords were established; the biggest trick is avoiding multiple references to the same story under different subject headings. Given the time period under study, I was also concerned with changes in keywords reflecting the shifting historical and social context. Keywords used in the search included bank deposits, bank reserves, banking law, banks and banking, building and loan associations, Federal Deposit Insurance Corporation, Federal Reserve system, and savings and loans. Care was taken to avoid double-counting entries that appeared under more than one keyword category.

The second task, coding the tone of the story, was a bit more involved and required several dry runs to work out kinks and settle on firm decision rules. Stories were coded based on the title entry in the *Reader's Guide*. They were coded as positive or negative from the vantage of the financial industry. For example, stories that mentioned bank failures, lax regulation, or consumer dissatisfaction were coded negative (1,033 stories, or 21 percent). Those that lauded innovation, spoke of banks as engines of economic growth, or offered features on particular banks and their managers were coded positive (566, or 11 percent). The majority of stories fell into the neutral or unable-to-code category (68 percent). The percent of articles coded identically by two coders was 94 percent.

TABLE 3.2 Participation Profiles—House

Year	Political Variation	Number of Hearings	Total Number Witnesses	Banks (%)	Bank Regulators (%)	Exec Branch (%)	Member of Congress (%)	Academics (%)	Other Regulators (%)	State Officials (%)	Other IGs (%)
1920	B	6	37	51	22	3	15	0	3	3	3
1922	B	6	58	50	15	19	8	0	2	0	9
1924	B	1	15	47	27		0	0	15	13	13
1926	C	2	33	6	39	6	0	21	6	0	21
1928	C	3	45	31	18	4	4	13	0	22	7
1930	B	2	36	47	14	0	17	0	0	8	14
1932	B	5	56	50	7	4	20	2	4	2	12
1934	C	3	39	13	10	3	18	30	0	13	13
1936	C	6	20	5	40	5	25	0	0	5	20
1938	C	5	24	12	21	0	12	29	0	17	8
1940	B	1	12	50	17	8	8	0	0	8	8
1942	B	0	0	0	0	0	0	0	0	0	0
1944	B	2	32	34	25	0	25	0	0	9	6
1946	B	1	3	33	33	0	33	0	0	0	0
1948	B	8	60	43	25	5	8	2	0	0	15
1950	C	4	68	18	15	3	10	0	18	3	34
1952	B	1	4	50	50		0	0	0	0	0
1954	B	2	7	0	86	14	0	0	0	0	0
1956	B	5	28	46	21	4	7	0	4	0	18
1958	B	3	48	54	15	0	15	0	2	2	12
1960	B	9	70	46	24	1	24	0	1	1	1
1962	B	6	29	55	28	10	3	0	0	3	0
1964	C	11	171	30	21	1	9	13	1	11	14
1966	B	12	161	40	25	2	6	6	2	6	10
1968	B	13	92	46	25	5	5	1	0	4	13
1970	C	6	113	36	9	2	3	8	10	2	31
1972	C	4	46	39	13	4	0	20	7	0	17
1974	B	5	78	62	15	4	0	0	6	0	13
1976	C	20	309	27	12	3	3	6	4	5	39
1978	C	11	242	41	10	1	3	1	6	15	24
1980	C	13	185	36	15	3	9	4	1	9	23
1982	C	13	112	37	13	3	8	3	4	3	29
1984	C	11	167	33	13	2	5	11	4	4	27
1986	C	11	139	24	31	1	8	6	1	7	22
1988	C	10	73	36	16	3	0	7	4	1	33

Note: B = Bank-dominant coalition; C = Competitive coalitions; n = 2612 witnesses, 231 hearings.

Year	Political Variation	Number of Hearings	Total Number Witnesses	Banks (%)	Bank Regulators (%)	Exec Branch (%)	Member of Congress (%)	Academics (%)	Other Regulators (%)	State Officials (%)	Other IGs (%)
1920	C	4	11	36	9	0	9	18	0	0	27
1922	C	6	49	14	16	0	20	2	12	0	35
1924	B	2	25	48	12	4	20	0	4	0	12
1926	B	1	29	93	0	3	0	3	0	0	0
1928	C	2	12	0	25	0	8	17	0	0	50
1930	C	1	10	0	40	0	20	0	0	0	40
1932	T	6	133	64	5	0	1	1	3	0	26
1934	C	5	56	46	9	0	4	2	0	5	34
1936	C	7	126	29	17	1	9	2	3	2	38
1938	C	4	35	48	11	6	11	2	6	0	17
1940	C	4	26	15	42	4	15	0	0	0	23
1942	B	0	0	0	0	0	0	0	0	0	0
1944	B	4	66	79	11	0	2	0	3	3	3
1946	B	2	3	33	66	0	0	0	0	0	0
1948	B	5	25	60	20	8	8	0	4	0	0
1950	B	5	42	64	17	7	7	0	0	5	0
1952	B	2	14	57	14	0	0	0	0	29	0
1954	B	4	52	69	14	2	0	2	0	8	6
1956	B	5	64	61	13	0	3	0	3	3	17
1958	B	1	10	70	10	0	10	0	0	10	0
1960	B	8	79	46	23	2	1	1	0	4	23
1962	C	7	80	29	9	4	3	5	0	6	34
1964	C	4	145	28	3	0	2	1	11	11	55
1966	B	9	132	52	9	4	11	4	1	6	14
1968	C	12	114	34	12	4	4	8	1	9	28
1970	C	10	208	36	7	1	4	3	3	7	39
1972	B	4	43	53	23	3	2	2	0	7	9
1974	T	13	184	40	14	3	1	16	2	8	17
1976	C	21	305	27	15	1	2	11	5	14	25
1978	C	12	202	36	17	2	1	5	4	10	24
1980	B	16	180	31	28	2	2	6	6	6	19
1982	C	7	206	29	12	2	5	3	4	11	34
1984	C	8	205	29	13	3	0	3	3	10	37
1986	C	8	134	32	20	1	3	1	1	3	38
1988	C	14	143	29	15	2	4	5	4	8	32

Note: B = Bank-dominant coalition; C = Competitive coalition; T = Transitory coalition; n = 3137 witnesses, 225 hearings.

Doing the Legislative Mambo: The Treatment of Legislation, 1919–1988

Once it has been established that participation in the financial subsystem varies over time, the task becomes understanding the impact of political variation on the policy process. The "policy stages" heuristic is a useful way of sorting out the myriad activities associated with the policy process (Jones 1984). In this chapter the focus is on the variety of legislative activities associated with agenda setting and policy adoption.

SETTING THE AGENDA IN CONGRESS

Agenda setting determines, in large part, the parameters of the policy debate. An agenda is simply a list of items of concern to someone. Most students of agenda setting build on the work of Cobb and Elder (1983), who identified three types of agendas—public, systemic, and decision. The public agenda is a list of items of concern to the public at large and is often delineated via content analysis of mass media outlets. In Chapter 3, I examined the relationship between increasing public salience and subsystem politics. The question then becomes, What effect does heightened public salience have on the government and decision agendas? Some argue the impact is direct, with "hot button," or highly salient, issues on the public agenda moving onto the government agenda. In this view legislators, the president, even the courts, respond to increased public concern by adding an item to their agenda.

For present purposes bill introduction in the House and Senate serves as an indicator of items on the government agenda. Quite simply, if members of Congress are concerned enough with a problem, they will more than likely offer a legislative solution. Bill introduction, although requiring resources, is a viable option for most legislators. It serves as a means of alerting oversight committees that all is not well, signals agency personnel, and often calms constituents who are demanding action.

The decision agenda is a subset of items from the government agenda that are up for active consideration. That is, they are problems that government players are actually trying to solve. Hearings and bills reported out of committee are used as an indicator of items on the decision agenda. Hearings, as discussed in Chapter 3, serve a variety of purposes. They allow committee members to probe the policy waters, facilitate communications among subsystem insiders and in some cases outsiders, and may serve as a mechanism for dispute resolution short of legislation. Thus hearings are intimately associated with the decision agenda. Hearings may also result in legislation being reported out of committee, a clear sign that an item has worked its way onto the decision agenda and is moving closer to adoption.

Agenda setting, then, is intimately tied to the legislative process.[1] The complete "dance of the legislature" encompasses several discrete events—bill introduction, the referral of legislation to committee, hearings, the reporting of legislation from committee, and floor activity. These various activities are both the heart and soul of the legislative process and key determinants of winners and losers in the policy game. Given the legislative locus of much of agenda building and policy adoption, an understanding of the committee system in Congress is essential.

Congressional committees are the central locus of action in the legislative process. Congress as an institution developed the committee system as a means of dividing policy responsibilities among legislators. Committees come to think of a particular policy domain as their turf (Shepsle 1978). Agenda setting requires one to maneuver legislation through committee so that it can be considered by the chamber as a whole. Committees perform a gate-keeping function, picking and choosing from items on the government agenda the few that will make it onto the decision agenda. They do this through hearings, markups, and finally by voting to send a bill to the floor. Among the most important influences on the performance of this gate-keeping function is the membership of the committee itself.

Committee membership, although subject to institutional constraints, is primarily determined by member interest in a particular policy area or reelection or a combination of the two (Hall and Groffman 1990; Fenno 1973; Jones, Baumgartner, and Talbert 1993). Member self-selection for committee assignments produces committees composed of experts, interesteds, and advocates. The result is that "policymaking within committees generally devolves to those interested in the policy area of question" (Jones, Baumgartner, and Talbert 1993, 658).

Many have assumed that the role of committees in the legislative process and the nature of committee membership give rise to a committee system, and by inference a policy process, that is static, that is, a system in which the nature of committee membership is fixed. Committees are composed of preference outliers whose policy preferences are not representative of the chamber as a whole. Such a system, in which the floor defers to committees in the formation and passage of legislation, thus biases the legislative process. The result is a system, in short, in which subsystem preferences reign supreme because committees act in a hegemonic fashion.

The case study of the formation of the Federal Reserve system, especially the New Deal restructuring of the system, brings this contention into doubt. Rather than committees acting as hegemons and subsystem preferences automatically being translated into programmatic form, subsystem and committee autonomy varies over time. Variation in committee autonomy is associated with both committee composition and change in subsystem politics. This chapter examines the impact of subsystem political variation on the treatment of legislation in the House and Senate between 1919 and 1988 (the 66th through the 100th Congress).[2] The chapter examines all domestic financial intermediary–related legislation introduced in Congress, as well as any legislation dealing with Federal Reserve monetary policy. It also examines any hearing dealing with such legislation and any hearing dealing with domestic financial intermediaries, whether such hearings are held by the banking committees or in another venue.

SALIENCE ON THE PUBLIC AGENDA, BILL INTRODUCTION, AND HEARINGS

In Chapter 3, I discussed the relationship between salience on the public agenda and subsystem political variation. Having found that increased public attention to financial regulation goes hand in hand with increased outsider participation in the financial subsystem, I move on to consider the impact of heightened public attention on government agenda building.

Table 4.1 demonstrates that increasing media attention is positively correlated with increased bill introduction. It appears that when an issue becomes hot on the public agenda, members of Congress are inclined to include it on the government agenda. What is true for Congress as a whole also holds for each chamber— bill introduction is positively correlated with issue salience. What is interesting about salience and bill introduction is the differing effect of public-agenda salience on committee and noncommittee legislators in the two chambers. In the House, public salience is most strongly associated with bill introduction by non–Banking Committee legislators. That is, it appears to attract outsiders to the business of financial regulation. In the Senate, the reverse is true—salience has a stronger effect on Banking Committee legislators.

TABLE 4.1 Salience and Bill Introduction, 1919–1988 (correlation between story counts and sponsorship)

	Bills (Total)	Committee Sponsored	Noncommittee Sponsored
House	.63	.53	.67
Senate	.69	.67	.48
Congress	.69	.60	.71

Note: All correlations are significant at $p < .001$.

Increasing public attention to banking matters also has an impact on events on the decision agenda. Increased salience is strongly correlated with the decision to hold hearings on banking matters in Congress as a whole, as well as in the House and Senate (see Table 4.2). The number of witnesses at hearings is also positively correlated with increased salience on the public agenda. Thus public salience also appears to influence events associated with the decision agenda.

When one controls for variation associated with the two major types of subsystem politics—dominant and competitive coalitions—interesting differences appear. In the House (see Table 4.3), the decision agenda of bank-dominant subsystems is less affected than that of competitive subsystems by events on the public agenda (the correlation is weak and not significant). Still, increased public salience, especially negative coverage, is correlated with an increase in the number and diversity of witnesses invited to testify at hearings.[3] Both the number of hearings and witnesses in competitive coalitions are strongly correlated with public-agenda salience.

In the Senate almost the opposite relationship holds. Both the number of hearings and witnesses under bank-dominant politics are more strongly correlated with public-agenda salience than is the case under competitive coalitions (Table 4.4), although variation associated with the tone of coverage is much like the House case—increasingly negative coverage is strongly correlated with an increase in the number of hearings and witnesses.

TABLE 4.2   Salience, Hearings, and Number of Witnesses, 1919–1988 (correlations reported are with story counts)

	Hearings	Witnesses
House	.58	.57
Senate	.54	.67
Congress	.60	.66

Note: All correlations are significant at $p < .001$.

TABLE 4.3   Subsystem Variation, Salience, Hearings, and Number of Witnesses—House, 1919–1988

	Hearings		Witnesses	
	Mean	Correlation	Mean	Correlation
Bank-dominant	5.6	.21	51.4	.42[a]
Competitive	8.3	.59[b]	111.9	.42[c]

[a] significant at $p < .12$.
[b] significant at $p < .02$.
[c] significant at $p < .10$.

TABLE 4.4   Subsystem Variation, Salience, Hearings, and Number of Witnesses—Senate, 1919–1988

	Hearings		Witnesses	
	Mean	Correlation	Mean	Correlation
Bank-dominant	4.7	.83[a]	53	.80[a]
Competitive	7.7	.36[b]	114.3	.57[c]

[a] significant at p < .001.
[b] significant at p < .14.
[c] significant at p < .01.

Finally, in both the House and the Senate the mean number of hearings and witnesses vary with subsystem political variation (Tables 4.3 and 4.4). Bank-dominant coalitions hold fewer hearings with fewer witnesses than do competitive coalitions. This reinforces the notion that bank-dominant politics present higher barriers to entry than is the case in competitive politics. Clearly, the subsystem appears to be opening up in the latter instance. The following section examines the impact of this phenomenon on bill introduction.

BILL SPONSORSHIP

Bill introduction in the House and Senate mark the entrance of an issue onto the government agenda. As such it is the first salvo fired in the policy process. Bill introduction is an important indicator of congressional interest in a particular program or policy area. Under bank-dominant coalitions, committees commit to "mutual noninterference pacts," in which other committees and legislators not a part of the committee stay out of committee business. In such a situation bill introduction is monopolized by members of the oversight committee. In contrast, in competitive and transitory coalitions, more and more noncommittee legislators try their hand at agenda setting vis-à-vis bill introduction.

The primary concern of this section is identifying the origin and destination of legislative proposals dealing with financial regulation. I am interested in three aspects of bill introduction: how the presence of interesteds on the committee affects the introduction of legislation, how sponsorship is affected by alterations in subsystem politics, and attempts to alter the venue in which banking regulation is considered.

Remember, interesteds are those Banking Committee members who have a background in the financial industry. In the case of regulatory legislation, one would expect the percentage of interesteds on the committee to be negatively correlated with bill introduction. This expectation is in line with the assumption that the financial industry has what it wants in the way of regulation and committee members with a background in the financial industry are loath to alter the status quo. Similarly, one would expect interested committee members to introduce less legislation, on average, than noninterested committee members. Interesteds, primarily motivated by self-interest, favor the status quo. Noninteresteds are more likely to pursue what they believe is good policy, which often involves tinkering with existing programs in pursuit of the public interest.

Subsystem members' ability to control the agenda should be strongly correlated with their ability to restrict participation at hearings. Thus under the bank-dominant scenario, bill introduction is dominated by committee members, and in competing and transitory coalitions a larger proportion of bills is introduced by noncommittee members. Bill introduction, then, indicates that an issue has worked its way onto the government agenda. As such, bill counts serve as an indicator of issue salience in Congress. That is, bills indicate an interest in, and awareness of, particular programs and policy areas by members of Congress (Leyden 1995; Baumgartner and Jones 1993). By distinguishing legislation sponsored by members of the banking committees from that sponsored by nonmembers, one gets a feel for issue salience on the banking committees and in the chamber as a whole.

Similar to the case with bill introduction, attempts to alter the venue or committee jurisdiction in which financial regulatory questions are considered should increase as one moves from the bank-dominant scenario to the more divisive politics of competitive coalitions. Venue switching is a significant challenge to subsystem autonomy, not to mention a serious breach of long-standing congressional norms. Baumgartner and Jones (1993) and Jones, Baumgartner, and Talbert (1993) suggest that venue switching occurs periodically, producing a punctuated equilibrium. That is, subsystem control (equilibrium) may be the norm for extended periods, but it is subject to challenge and, if the challenge is successful, change. What I suggest is that change most often takes the form of variation in subsystem politics rather than dissolution of subsystem arrangements. Hence, subsystem arrangements produce a wavering equilibrium, as evidenced by attempts at venue switching and policy responses by oversight committees that head off such challenges.

The preceding gives rise to the following hypotheses:

Hypothesis 4.1: Interesteds, and committees dominated by interesteds, will introduce less legislation on average than noninterested committee members or committees dominated by noninteresteds.
Hypothesis 4.2: The fraction of bills introduced by outsiders (non–Banking Committee legislators) will increase as politics shifts from bank-dominant to competitive coalitions.
Hypothesis 4.3: The fraction of bills referred to committees other than banking will increase as politics shifts from bank-dominant to competitive coalitions.

To begin, banking committee members introduce the majority of legislation dealing with financial regulation, exercising relatively tighter control in the Senate (see the total in Table 4.5). This interchamber difference in the degree of control is also evident in the role played by chairs as sponsors. In the House, chairs sponsor 26 percent of committee-sponsored legislation and 16 percent of all legislation. The Senate figure for chairs is 40 percent of member-sponsored and 25 percent of all banking legislation. It appears, then, that the Senate Banking Committee and its chair are more active as agenda setters than their House counterparts.

Interested committee members do not appear to be especially active as sponsors of regulatory legislation. The correlation between the percentage of interesteds on the banking committees and the number of bills introduced by committee members is negative and relatively strong in both the Senate, −.53, and the House, −.63. What happens when the interested is also a chair? In both the House and Senate interested chairs introduce a smaller fraction of legislation than noninterested chairs—23 percent compared to 27 percent in the House and 33 percent compared to 41 percent in the Senate. Thus interested chairs are less active as sponsors, the larger decline being in the Senate. Still, the role of the chair and the gate-keeping functions associated with it seem to mitigate against chairs adopting the slowdown tactic of interesteds in general.

The findings in Table 4.5 indicate that Banking Committee members' control over bill introduction slips under competitive coalitions (offering support for hypothesis 4.2). Combine this with the effects of salience, and it appears that as banking becomes the subject of increased public scrutiny, more and more outsiders become involved in attempts to set the banking agenda in Congress.

TABLE 4.5   Bill Sponsorship and Referral, 1919–1988

	House		Senate	
Subsystem Politics	*Committee Sponsored (%)*	*Referred to non-Banking Committee (%)*	*Committee Sponsored (%)*	*Referred to non-Banking Committee (%)*
Bank-dominant	59	4.2	69	6
Competitive	53	15.9	58	11.7
Transitory			70	4.5
Total	55[a]	11.1[b]	62[c]	10[d]
	n = 2949		n = 1210	

[a] Gamma = .10; chi squared (1 d.f.) = 7.37 (p < .01).
[b] Gamma = −.63; chi squared (1 d.f.) = 104.18 (p < .001).
[c] Gamma = .23; chi squared (2 d.f.) = 15.21 (p < .001).
[d] Gamma = −.35; chi squared (2 d.f.) = 11.82 (p < .001).

Similarly, the fraction of bills referred to committees other than the House or Senate Banking Committee climbs dramatically when one compares bank-dominant to competitive coalitions (supporting hypothesis 4.3). Outsiders are clearly attempting to alter the venue of the conflict under competitive coalitions. Interesting enough, the transitory scenario in the Senate involves a decline in venue switching and noncommittee-sponsored legislation. It appears that for the most part challengers are either willing to work with the committees or unable to muster the resources necessary to alter the venue. This may very well have something to do with the nature of outsider involvement under transitory politics—outsiders are quite often temporary sojourners with no strong interest group affiliation.[4] Under the transitory scenario outsiders are also faced with a strong insider presence, which works to encourage them to stick with the established rules and norms of the legislative process. That is, they respect committee turf, preferring to work with the system rather than against it.

COMMITTEE DECISIONS AND SUBSYSTEM AUTONOMY

If bill introduction serves as an indicator of entrance onto the government agenda, what the committee does with the bill—does it hold hearings? does it report the bill out of committee favorably?—determines its fate on the decision agenda. It also sets the stage for the activity associated with policy adoption—amendments from the floor and passage as law.

Reporting Legislation from Committee

Subsystems theory suggests that bills introduced into an environment characterized by conflict, such as that which exists under competitive coalitions, would have less chance of being reported out of committee than those introduced into an environment marked by consensus—for example, bank-dominant coalitions. This hypothesis is tested through an examination of the fate of legislative proposals introduced in each type of subsystem.

  Hypothesis 4.4: The fraction of bills reported out of committee will decline
     as one moves from bank-dominant to competitive coalitions.
  Hypothesis 4.5: The fraction of bills amended in committee will increase as
     one moves from bank-dominant to competitive coalitions.

Before we examine committee activity, it is important to get a feel for who is sponsoring the legislation eventually reported out of committee. Ninety-five percent of the legislation reported out of the Banking Committee in the House is sponsored by committee members, compared to 85 percent in the Senate. Chairs are sponsors of 67 percent of the legislation reported out of the House Banking Committee, compared to 53 percent in the Senate. Thus although sponsorship of legislation may vary with subsystem politics, positive action by the Banking Committee is strongly correlated with the identity of legislative sponsors. Chairs are instrumental in steering legislation through committee, and committee membership appears to be a near requisite for successful sponsorship. Thus committee members tightly control policy formulation and movement of legislative proposals toward the floor.

Columns 1 and 3 of Table 4.6 contain the percentage of bills reported out of the House and Senate committees, respectively. As expected, bank-dominant subsystems report a larger fraction of legislation out of committee than do competitive subsystems (offering support for hypothesis 4.4). The transitory scenario in the Senate is indistinguishable from the bank-dominant case, suggesting that the temporary involvement of some outsiders does not necessarily lead to stalemate.

Similarly, amendment activity increases as one moves from bank-dominant to competitive politics (columns 2 and 4 in Table 4.6). Thus in the competitive scenario, even though outsiders are a significant presence, they are still players in the *financial* subsystem. The increased level of amendments offered in committee could mean either of two things. In the first scenario outsiders' legislative proposals are subject to financial-industry scrutiny and amendment. A second possibility is that outsiders are acting as amenders of financial-industry proposals. In all likelihood, both are occurring. The transitory-coalition scenario in the Senate demonstrates that in the absence of well-organized interests—either banks or competitors— amendment activity increases dramatically. It appears that committee members are trolling the policy waters, adding any- and everything to legislation in hopes of pleasing someone.

Floor Amendments and Passage into Law

Many writing in the subsystem tradition assume the larger political system exercises a uniform effect on a subsystem.[5] That is, it contains broad parameters that constrain activity, and during economic, political, or environmental crises, it may even directly shape subsystem activity. I suggest that whereas subsystems in general

TABLE 4.6 Legislation Reported from Committee, 1919–1988 (percentages)

	House		Senate	
	Reported from Committee	With Amendment	Reported from Committee	With Amendment
Bank-dominant	8.4	37	21.2	38
Competitive	5.4	67	13.2	46
Transitory			20.4	68
	n = 2949[a]	n = 193[b]	n = 1210[c]	n = 193[d]

[a] Gamma = .23; chi squared (1 d.f.) = 10.35; p < .001.
[b] Gamma = .39; chi squared (1 d.f.) = 5.52; p < .02.
[c] Gamma = .25; chi squared (2 d.f.) = 12.35; p < .001.
[d] Gamma = .10; chi squared (2 d.f.) = 5.49; p < .06.

are fairly autonomous, autonomy is itself affected by subsystem political varia-tion. This section tests that proposition through a focus on floor amendments and the passage of legislation as law.

This final section, then, is concerned with the extent to which the parent house acts as an impediment to decisions reached in committee. Subsystem autonomy is operationalized as the ability of the Banking Committee to steer legislation through the minefield that is the parent chamber. Autonomy is measured in two ways. In the first instance, autonomy is operationalized as the ability of the committee to mini-mize amendments from the floor. The second measure of autonomy focuses on the ability of the committee to secure the enshrinement of legislation into law.

An important feature of subsystems is their ability to set the agenda and formu-late policy with little or no interference from outsiders. Subsystems theorists argue that policy is "formulated or implemented . . . with scant attention from actors in other subsystems, much less the public at large" (Davidson 1977, 105). Yet this au-tonomy should vary with a change in subsystem politics. The bank-dominant sce-nario envisions the legislative process as "logrolling." Quite simply, committees enjoy a high degree of autonomy in the formulation and passage of legislation be-cause noncommittee legislators defer to committee members. Thus one would ex-pect a larger proportion of bills originating under bank-dominant-coalition con-ditions to be passed on the floor without amendment than those introduced under competitive or transitory coalitions. This is because the committee presents a united front in the former but is divided or apparently rudderless in the latter.

Hypothesis 4.6: Amendments from the floor will increase as one moves from bank-dominant toward competitive coalitions.

Finally, the fraction of legislation enacted into law should decrease as one moves from bank-dominant to competitive coalitions. The bicameral nature of the legislature, as well as the "natural predilection" of the banking committees, explains this phenomenon. First, the banking committees by their very nature (their membership, relations with clientele, and history) are more comfortable with the bank-dominant scenario than with the others. This means they are more inclined to act as advocates of legislation hatched in the bank-dominant setting. In addition, committee autonomy involves not just the parent chamber as a hur-dle but the other chamber as well. Legislation coming out of the more conflictual scenarios—transitory and competitive—is bound to meet a rockier reception when it gets to the other chamber. This is because losers in the home chamber will be waiting for them, especially if the losers are financial-industry actors.

Hypothesis 4.7: The fraction of legislation enacted into law will decrease as one moves from bank-dominant toward competitive coalitions.

Table 4.7 contains the amendment rate for legislation reported out of commit-tee in the House and Senate. Most interesting is the interchamber difference when it comes to comparing bank-dominant and competitive coalitions. The relationship is much as expected in both chambers—bills introduced in the competitive scenario are subject to more amendments than those under bank-dominant conditions—but the difference is smaller in the Senate. It appears that the committees are less able, or perhaps less inclined, to preserve the "legislative purity" of reported legislation under competitive conditions. When politics become seemingly rudderless, as they do under transitory coalitions in the Senate, everybody and their brother becomes involved. Indeed, nearly all the legislation reported out under transitory coalitions is subject to amendment on the floor.

The final test of subsystem autonomy is the committee's ability to shepherd a bill through the legislative gauntlet and get it signed into law. As predicted, committees operating in a bank-dominant setting are more successful at this challenge on the whole (Table 4.8). The higher success rate of the bank-dominant coalition reinforces the notion that bank-dominant politics is viewed as the norm not just by Banking Committee legislators but by legislators in the chamber as a whole. Under bank-dominant conditions the committees exercise a good deal of influence over the ultimate prize—the passage of legislation into law.

THE LEGISLATIVE MAMBO IN THE SENATE AND HOUSE: A SUMMARY

Perhaps the most important conclusion drawn from the preceding is that Banking Committee members play a key role in policy initiation and formation in the

TABLE 4.7   Subsystem Autonomy—Floor Amendment Activity, 1919–1988 (percent of legislation passed that was amended on the floor)

Politics	House	Senate
Bank-dominant	46	39
Competitive	67	47
Transitory		92
	n = 134[a]	n = 145[b]

[a] Gamma = .24; chi squared (1 d.f.) = 2.76; p < .10.
[b] Gamma = .06; chi squared (2 d.f.) = 11.83; p < .001.

TABLE 4.8   Subsystem Autonomy—Law, 1919–1988 (percent of total legislation passed into law)

Politics	House[a]	Senate[b]
Bank-dominant	4.0	11.4
Competitive	2.6	5.9

[a] Gamma = .21; chi squared (1 d.f.) = 3.83; p < .05.
[b] Gamma = .34; chi squared (1 d.f.) = 8.83; p < .001.

financial subsystem. That said, we need to consider influences on committee members as well as variation in what they do associated with subsystem politics. An important determinant of agenda activity is media attention. Salience is positively associated with bill introduction, hearings, and the number of witnesses at hearings, although its impact on Banking Committee members varies by chamber.

Banking Committee legislators dominate agenda setting under the bank-dominant scenario, and outsiders grab a bigger piece of the agenda-setting spotlight under competitive coalitions. Interesteds appear to work to slow down the introduction of legislation no matter the politics of the subsystem. Committee member sponsorship, no matter the particular variant of subsystem politics, appears to be an essential ingredient in getting a bill reported and enacted into law. Clearly, committee members act as gatekeepers in the legislative process. Senate chairs are more active in this role than their House counterparts, but regardless of chamber the chair is a valuable ally in the legislative mambo.

Finally, variation in subsystem politics affects the production of legislation—reporting legislation from committee, amendment activity, and passage into law—in both chambers. Given that subsystem political variation affects the mechanics of the legislative process, it is now time to explore this phenomenon in greater detail. I am especially interested in how variation in subsystem politics shapes legislation. Does legislation produced in a setting dominated by interesteds and industry interests invariably favor the regulated industry? Do subsystems typical of bank-dominant coalitions produce legislation markedly different from that produced by competitive and transitory coalitions? What is the impact of extra-subsystem actors on the type of legislation produced? Chapter 5 addresses these questions through content analysis of the financial regulatory legislation produced by both chambers between 1919 and 1988.

5

Examining Inter-Subsystem Dynamics: Determining Who Benefits from Regulatory Legislation

This chapter picks up where Chapter 4 left off. Our attention is directed away from the mechanics of the legislative process toward the end result of committee activity. The focus is on the outputs, legislation and law, of committees operating in the different subsystem contexts. The chapter has two interrelated concerns. The first is discovering variation in the distribution of benefits associated with variation in politics. Quite simply, does policy output vary with a change in participation (subsystem politics)? The inquiry focuses on differences between bank-dominant and competitive coalitions. The second concern involves discovering whether the political variants—bank-dominant, transitory, and competitive coalitions—produce outputs as predicted by the models that dominate the literature. In order to get at these propositions I examine financial legislation produced in both chambers between 1919 (the 66th Congress) and 1988 (the 100th Congress).

WHAT'LL YOU HAVE?
POLICY TYPE AND SUBSYSTEM POLITICS

The central concern of the chapter, then, is determining who benefits from regulation. The models of subsystem politics reviewed in Chapter 1 suggest that the answer to the preceding is determined by the mix of actors participating in the subsystem. Subsystems produce three types of policy—distributive, redistributive, and regulatory. Under the bank-dominant scenario, policy is distributive. That is, all the private parties involved get something from whatever policy is reported out or passed as law, with the costs born by outsiders. The ability to strike such deals erodes as politics become more open to outsider participation or subject to environmental stress.

Models on the bank-dominant end of the continuum portray the regulated industry as a homogeneous entity; others suggest that industry unity varies across time and circumstances. One explanation offered for the decline in benefits accruing to the regulated concerns the degree of unity (and thus hegemony) among the industry in question. As industry unity weakens, factions within the industry seek benefits for themselves. What this means is that under the competing and transitory scenarios, policy is a mix of distributive policy; redistributive policy, with a segment of the financial industry securing benefits at the expense of another faction or outsiders gaining at the expense of insiders; and regulatory policy, in which regulators are given extended authority to police their increasingly unruly charges.

Thus as politics move away from the bank-dominant scenario, one would expect to find a larger share of benefits going to a segment of the financial industry as opposed to the share going to the industry as a whole, more legislation extending regulation, and more legislation benefiting nonsubsystem players. These expectations give rise to the following hypotheses:

Hypothesis 5.1: The fraction of legislation benefiting the regulated industry as a whole will decrease as one moves away from bank-dominant coalitions.

Hypothesis 5.2: The proportion of legislation that benefits a fraction of the regulated will increase as one moves from bank-dominant toward competitive coalitions.

Hypothesis 5.3: Nonindustry interests will enjoy more legislative benefits in the competitive-coalition setting than in the other subsystem types.

Hypothesis 5.4: The fraction of legislation extending regulatory authority will increase as one moves toward competitive coalitions.

In order to get at these propositions, I break the legislative process down into two parts, concentrating on an examination of the content of legislation in each section. Four dichotomous variables were created to determine the beneficiaries of legislation and law. The first category included all bills that extended benefits to all classes of financial-services intermediaries. Such distributive legislation was supported by all the major industry trade associations and financial regulators. A second category included legislation that was mildly redistributive in that it extended benefits to one financial-industry segment at the expense of another. A third category extended regulation. That is, it created anew, or reinforced, existing policing functions of financial regulators. A final variable included radically redistributive legislation that extended benefits to outsiders, often in the form of consumer-protection legislation, and in so doing limited what financial intermediaries could or could not do.

The first section examines the content of legislation reported out of committee. A total of 281 bills are reviewed—151 in the House and 130 in the Senate. This data set includes the complete set of bills reported out of the various House and Senate committees between 1919 and 1988 (see the appendix to this chapter for a detailed discussion of the data set and coding procedures). Following the examination of bills reported out of committee, we move on to consider the content of legislation enacted into law. The data set in the third section includes all bills reported from committee that are eventually enacted as law. A total of 131 bills are analyzed, 78 originating in the House and 53 from the Senate.

REPORTING LEGISLATION FROM COMMITTEE

This section focuses on a key stage of the legislative process—reporting a bill from committee. Bills examined in this section include all legislation dealing with the regulation of financial intermediaries that were reported out of any committee in the House and Senate. Before we move to a detailed examination of committee outputs in the various subsystem types, it will be useful to get a feel for the general nature of legislation reported out of committee. Table 5.1 sketches a rough portrait of the beneficiaries of financial legislation reported from committee in the House and Senate between 1919 and 1988. The figures in the table are percentages that represent the fraction of bills reported out of committee that contain some benefit for the interest identified in the column. So for example, 75 percent of the legislation reported from committee in the House and Senate extended benefits to the financial industry.

The table suggests that the financial subsystem operates as modeled by subsystem theory. The vast majority of legislation reported out of committee favors financial-industry actors. Still, a sizable portion of legislation reported out of committee extends benefits to outsiders with the Senate apparently more inclined to extend such benefits than the House. But what of variation in legislative outputs over time? Is the production of legislation shaped by variation in subsystem politics? We now turn to these questions.

Bill Production in the House

Venue switching, that is, an instance in which committees other than the Banking Committee deal with questions of financial regulation, is rare in the House. One hundred and thirty-one of the 151 bills reported out of committee involve the

TABLE 5.1   Legislation Reported from Committee Favoring Select Interests, 1919–1988

| Chamber of Origin | Legislation Favors | | | |
	Financial Industry	Financial- Industry Faction	Extending Regulation	Outsiders
House	75	59	37	34
Senate	73	43	33	42
Total n = 281	75	51	35	38

Note: Figures represent the fraction of legislation reported out of committee that extends benefits to a particular interest.

Banking Committee as the home venue. Nonbanking committees reporting out banking legislation occurs most often under competitive coalitions—sixteen of the twenty instances recorded.

A review of the data in Table 5.2 reveals that bank-dominant coalitions produce a little over twice as much legislation that extends benefits to the regulated (distributive policy) than extends regulation. Similarly, they tend to be especially stingy when it comes to providing benefits to outsiders or redistributing subsystem goodies. The ratio of policy favoring the financial industry to that favoring outsiders is over 4 to 1.

Policy takes a redistributive turn under competitive coalitions—the ratio of policy outputs favoring the financial industry to that favoring outsiders is 1.5 to 1. This redistributive trend is also stronger among subsystem insiders, with the ratio of legislation extending benefits to a particular financial-industry faction to the total industry nearing parity (compared to 1.5 to 1 under bank-dominant politics). Interestingly, the ratio of legislation extending regulation to that favoring the regulated remains nearly identical under competitive coalitions.

As predicted (hypothesis 5.1), the financial industry does better under bank-dominant coalitions, and outsiders improve their showing under competitive coalitions (hypothesis 5.3). There is a slight increase in the level of legislation benefiting a specific industry faction as one moves from bank-dominant to competitive coalitions, but it is not statistically significant. Finally, the fraction of regulatory legislation actually declines under competitive coalitions in the House. Apparently subsystem players involved in a competitive milieu are loath to seek a regulatory solution to their problems in the House.

Bill Production in the Senate

Rare in the House, venue switching is almost unheard of in the Senate. Only 1 of the 131 bills reported out of committee did not originate in the Banking Commit-

TABLE 5.2   Legislation Reported from Committee Favoring Select Interests—House, 1919–1988

Subsystem Politics	Legislation Favors			
	Financial Industry[a]	*Financial-Industry Faction*	*Extending Regulation*	*Outsiders*[b]
Bank-dominant	85	56	40	18
Competitive	68	60	35	45

n = 151

Note: Figures represent the fraction of legislation reported out of committee that extends benefits to a particular interest.

[a] Gamma = .47; chi squared (1 d.f.) = 5.86; p < .02.

[b] Gamma = −.59; chi squared (1 d.f.) = 11.93; p < .001.

tee. This suggests that institutional boundaries are more respected in the Senate—at least when it comes to hearings and reporting legislation out of committee—but it does not mean that Senate-based politics are more exclusionary when it comes to outsider demands.

Indeed, a review of Table 5.3 reveals that outsiders do comparatively better in every subsystem variant in the Senate than was the case in the House.[1] Under bank-dominant politics the ratio of legislation producing insider to outsider benefits is half that of the House (2.5 to 1). Not that insiders (bank-dominant coalitions) have gotten soft in the Senate. The ratio of distributive legislation (that favoring the regulated industry) to regulatory legislation is nearly 4 to 1.

As is the case in the House, politics are markedly more redistributive under competitive coalitions. The ratio of insider to outsider benefits declines under both competitive and transitory coalitions, as does the financial industry to financial-industry faction ratio. Legislation is also increasingly regulatory under transitory and competitive coalitions (as predicted by hypothesis 5.4).

Comparison between the two dominant-coalition variants offers support for all four hypotheses. As one moves from bank-dominant to competitive politics, the fraction of legislation benefiting the regulated declines. The decline in industrywide benefits is matched by an increase in faction-specific benefits as well as outsider benefits. Finally, competitive coalitions in the Senate produce more legislation of a regulatory nature than do bank-dominant coalitions. It is not so much that they are more active on this front than House-based competitive coalitions. Rather, House-based bank-dominant coalitions are hyperactive in this regard.

TABLE 5.3   Legislation Reported from Committee Favoring Select Interests—Senate, 1919–1988

| Subsystem Politics | Legislation Favors | | | |
	Financial Industry[a]	Financial-Industry Faction[b]	Extending Regulation[c]	Outsiders[d]
Bank-dominant	82	33	23	31
Transitory	77	50	42	36
Competitive	68	47	37	49

n = 130

Note: Figures represent the fraction of legislation reported out of committee that extends benefits to a particular interest. Tests of significance reflect a comparison of bank dominant and competitive types only (n = 120). The counts for transitory coalitions were so small as to make the reported statistics for all three suspect.

[a] Gamma = .37; chi squared (1 d.f.) = 2.70; $p < .10$.
[b] Gamma = −.29; chi squared (1 d.f.) = 2.11; $p < .15$.
[c] Gamma = −.33; chi squared (1 d.f.) = 2.36; $p < .12$.
[d] Gamma = −.37; chi squared (1 d.f.) = 3.68; $p < .06$.

As the preceding review indicates, bill production in the House and Senate are remarkably similar. Policy outputs in the Senate and House vary according to subsystem politics. In general each political variation performs as expected. That is, the beneficiaries of legislation reported out of committee are as the models would predict. The following section examines the end product of the policy process originating in committees in the House and Senate, the passage of legislation into law.

THE CONTENT OF LAW

This section concerns how the chamber of origin and the other chamber affect legislation reported out of committee. We get at this through indirect means, examining the content of legislation enacted as law (see the appendix to this chapter for a detailed discussion of the data set). Table 5.4 displays the distribution of benefits in legislation eventually enacted into law. The findings of the previous section appear to hold nearly constant in the case of legislation passed into law. That is, the majority of legislation produced and enacted into law assumes a distributive format, benefiting the financial-industry members of the subsystem. As was the case at the reporting stage, outsiders enjoy a higher rate of success in the Senate. One difference from the reporting stage involves the fraction of regulatory legislation that becomes law. The Senate actually produces a higher percentage of law that extends regulation than does the House, the reverse of what occurred at the reporting stage.

Tables 5.5 and 5.6 detail the beneficiaries of laws originating in the House and Senate, respectively.[2] When we compare the distribution of benefits within each political variant, the results are as expected. Under the bank-dominant scenario the regulated are major beneficiaries of law. Indeed, the ratio of distributive to regulatory legislation is a little over 2 to 1 in the House and nearly 4 to 1 in the Senate. Similarly, those with radical redistribution on their mind would be better off looking elsewhere. The ratio of insider to outsider benefits is around 4 to 1 in

TABLE 5.4   Law Favoring Select Interests, 1919–1988

Chamber of Origin	Legislation Favors			
	Financial Industry	Financial- Industry Faction	Extending Regulation	Outsiders
House	75	58	28	33
Senate	75	40	36	38
Total	75	49	30	35
n = 131				

Note: Figures represent the fraction of law that favors a particular interest.

TABLE 5.5   Law Favoring Select Interests—House, 1919–1988

Subsystem Politics	Legislation Favors			
	Financial Industry	*Financial- Industry Faction*	*Extending Regulation*[a]	*Outsiders*[b]
Bank-dominant	78	53	36	19
Competitive	74	62	21	45
n = 78				

Note: Figures represent the fraction of legislation reported out of committee that extends benefits to a particular interest.

[a] Gamma = .35; chi squared (1 d.f.) = 2.06; $p < .15$.

[b] Gamma = −.55; chi squared (1 d.f.) = 5.31; $p < .02$.

TABLE 5.6   Law Favoring Select Interests—Senate, 1919–1988

Subsystem Politics	Legislation Favors			
	Financial Industry	*Financial- Industry Faction*	*Extending Regulation*[a]	*Outsiders*[b]
Bank-dominant	79	32	21	21
Transitory	67	33	33	67
Competitive	74	42	42	42
n = 53				

Note: Figures represent the fraction of legislation reported out of committee that extends benefits to a particular interest. Tests of significance reflect a comparison of bank dominant and competitive types only (n = 50). The counts for transitory coalitions were so small as to make the reported statistics for all three suspect.

[a] Gamma = −.51; chi squared (1 d.f.) = 2.97; $p < .08$.

[b] Gamma = −.51; chi squared (1 d.f.) = 2.97; $p < .08$.

both chambers, although the House is more willing than the Senate to produce more mildly redistributive policy, legislation that benefits one financial-industry faction at the expense of another. Outsiders do relatively better under transitory and competing coalitions, although the regulated are still the major beneficiaries of law. The ratio of distributive to redistributive legislation drops to under half of what it was in the bank-dominant scenario in both the House and Senate. The proportion of legislation redistributing benefits to a financial-industry faction also increases under competitive coalitions, as does the proportion of regulatory legislation in the Senate.

The relationship between the two major political variants—bank-dominant and competitive—is much as expected. As predicted, bank-dominant scenarios produced more legislation favoring the entire financial industry, and competitive coalitions generate more redistributive legislation—with redistribution occurring both interindustry and with outsiders. Finally, the results concerning the extension of regulation are mixed. As was the case at the reporting stage in the House, competitive coalitions produce a good deal less regulatory legislation than do bank-dominant coalitions. The exact opposite holds true in the Senate.

Although the preceding offers fairly robust support for the proposition that competitive and bank-dominant politics produce different policy outcomes, it glosses over an important subsystem dynamic. Policy is the product of the joint endeavors of the House and Senate. In order to get at the interconnected element of the financial subsystem, subsystem politics were reclassified based on the politics of the two chambers. The easiest part involved those sessions in which House and Senate politics were identical—the coding remained unchanged. Those sessions in which one chamber was bank-dominant and the other was competitive were classified as transitory. If a session was transitory in either chamber it was classified as transitory.

Table 5.7 reinforces much of the preceding in the cases of bank-dominant and competitive coalitions. The financial industry as a whole does better in the bank-dominant scenario, and it does remarkably well under competitive politics as well. It is when the chambers are in turmoil, the transitory-coalition scenario, that the financial industry suffers its sharpest decline. Although the decline is relative, the financial industry manages to secure benefits in the majority of legislation passed. Still, the data in Table 5.7 illustrate the importance of a bicameral vantage of subsystem politics. Outsiders do markedly better when there is a significant interchamber difference in politics. The financial industry itself appears to be more factionalized under such conditions, and outsiders make their biggest gains.

TABLE 5.7   Law Favoring Select Interests—Congress, 1919–1988

Subsystem Politics	Legislation Favors			
	Financial Industry [a]	Financial-Industry Faction	Extending Regulation	Outsiders [b]
Bank-dominant	88	47	26	18
Transitory	67	54	30	46
Competitive	78	46	34	37

n = 131

Note: Figures represent the fraction of law that favors a particular interest.
[a] Gamma = .40; chi squared (2 d.f.) = 5.46; $p < .07$.
[b] Gamma = −.40; chi squared (2 d.f.) = 7.49; $p < .02$.

CONCLUSION

If the preceding offers any obvious lesson, it is that organized interests reign supreme in the financial subsystem. Only when outsiders organize and successfully challenge financial-industry hegemony do they receive substantial legislative benefits.

Identifying beneficiaries of regulatory legislation is a major concern of this chapter, but determining whether the measures developed in preceding chapters are meaningful representations of subsystem politics is perhaps the most important goal. Chapter 4 offered some support for the measure developed in Chapter 3, identifying variation in the level of legislative outputs, committee autonomy, and the like associated with changes in subsystem politics. This chapter demonstrates that the quality of legislative outputs varies with political change. Bank-dominant coalitions produce a disproportionate share of legislation that promotes the interests of the financial industry. The extension of regulatory authority is positively correlated with the decline in industry unity. Competitive and transitory coalitions produce a more dispersed distribution of benefits.

Chapters 3 and 4 offered a long-range view of life in the financial subsystem, a portrait painted with the broadest of strokes. Chapters 6 and 7 use case studies to get at the effects of subsystem political variation and changes in interest group participation in more detail. The focus is shifted to shorter time periods and includes a more detailed discussion of the impact of a variety of environmental variables on beliefs and the shape of policy outcomes in the financial subsystem.

APPENDIX

The first step in the evaluation process involved identifying those bills reported out of committee. This exercise was an extension of the bill search that produced the data set for Chapter 4. The *Congressional Record* details the legislative history of bills. The *Record* contains not only the sponsor of legislation and the committee to which it is referred but also tracks its fate, indicating whether legislation is reported from committee, is subject to amendment, and is passed in the chamber of origin, as well as its fate in the other chamber and if it is signed into law.

Copies of all bills reported out of committee were obtained from the House and Senate *Reports* for each session of Congress. In most cases the *Reports* indicate the changes made in standing legislation, usually by highlighting additions or deletions and discussing them in the *Report* itself. In some instances I had to go back and track the original legislation, either through earlier *Reports* or by using the *United States Statutes at Large*. *Reports* from both chambers were examined, as was the report issued by the Conference Committee in those cases in which a conference was called. The *United States Statutes at Large* was consulted to evaluate bills enacted into law.

Four dichotomous variables were constructed so as to identify beneficiaries of regulatory legislation. The first variable, X1, is coded 1 if the legislation under review favored any member of the regulated industry—primarily commercial banks and thrifts. This was a first attempt to distinguish legislation that extends benefits to the financial industry from that which does not. Early variations of subsystem models such as the iron triangle variant suggest that the majority of policy created in the subsystem setting favors the private interests who dominate the system. In this view, policy outputs are distributive in nature. The most powerful interest groups active in the subsystem secure a piece of the action vis-à-vis legislation. The determination of whether a piece of legislation extended benefits to the regulated was based on how the proposed legislation altered existing regulatory arrangements. Such a judgment is certainly subjective, but efforts were made to increase the reliability of the coding as follows. The first step involved reading the House or Senate *Report*. The *Reports* indicate not only the proposed changes in legislation but often contain a rationale for the changes. In some cases they also contain minority reports that object to proposed changes. These comments often identify the intended beneficiaries and, although not entirely objective, give one a feel for the intent of legislators. In addition to reading the reports, I consulted a variety of secondary sources—*Banker* magazine, the annual reports of the various regulatory agencies, the *New York Times*, and the like—to get a feel for the intentions of the authors of legislation as well as the probable outcome of regulatory change.

In order to increase the reliability of the coding exercise, I coded all legislation twice. The results were compared, and in the few cases in which there was a change in coding on any of the variables, less than 7 percent of all legislation reported out of committee (nineteen bills), further research was conducted on the legislation.

Legislation coded 1 in this case ranged from bills that relaxed previous restrictions on specific activities (increasing the ceiling on loan amounts to individual borrowers, reducing reserve requirements, or increasing deposit insurance [which was also coded as extending benefits to consumers or nonregulated actors]) to those that allowed the financial industry to engage in previously prohibited activity (the establishment of NOW accounts, the sale of securities or insurance, or the establishment of branches in the form of automatic teller machines [ATM]).

The second variable, $X2$, is actually a subset of the first variable. It is coded 1 if the legislation favored one segment of the regulated industry over another. The latter three in the preceding example are cases that were coded positive for both $X1$ and $X2$. This variable takes into account the divisions within the financial industry itself. Legislation that favored the interests of thrifts, credit unions, or commercial banks at the expense of the others, as well as legislation that favored one faction of a particular industry—small versus large banks, for example—was coded 1. Legislation loosening or tightening branching provisions is a nice example of the type of legislation that has an interindustry impact and favors larger institutions over their smaller brethren. Allowing commercial banks to increase loan amounts on real estate is an example of legislation that favors one type of financial actor, commercial banks, over another, thrifts.

Once again, the determination of whether legislation favored one faction of the regulated over another was fairly straightforward. This is due in no small part to the objections that usually accompany such legislation. Losers do not suffer in silence, voicing their complaints at hearings, in the press, or through members of the banking committees in the form of dissenting comments in the *Report* containing the bill. *Banker* magazine, the *New York Times*, and the transcripts of hearings were especially helpful in the coding process.

The third variable, $X3$, is coded 1 if the legislation extends regulatory authority. Coding in this case is fairly simple. Legislation that creates new regulatory responsibilities or establishes a new regulatory agency is coded 1. For example, HR 9915—originating in the

73rd Congress—gave the FDIC authority to approve or disapprove mergers, consolidations, or the assumption of deposit liabilities involving banks with insured deposits.

Some acts were coded 1 for both X1 and X3. A nice example is the National Bank Act of 1933, which extended regulatory authority in a variety of areas—empowering the OCC to appoint conservators of insolvent banks, charging the Federal Reserve with controlling (and restricting) the use of bank credit for speculative purposes, or allowing the OCC and Fed to remove the management of troubled banks. At the same time the act allowed banks to issue preferred stock not subject to individual liability, providing them with a means of raising capital not previously available to commercial banks.

The fourth variable, X4, is coded 1 if the bill contains benefits for nonregulated interest groups. A majority of these bills contain consumer-protection provisions, such as legislation requiring banks to reveal compound interest rates on loans and a variety of truth-in-lending provisions. They also include bills that prevent, curtail, or turn back the expansion of the regulated into new economic endeavors such as insurance underwriting or securities brokerage.

6

Green Grass and High Tides Forever: Regulating Bank Holding Companies

The passage of bank holding-company legislation is traditionally portrayed as the extension of financial regulation to banks and businesses evading New Deal prohibitions on branching and investment activity. In this view, the passage of the Bank Holding Company Act of 1956 was a triumph of New Deal regulation. I offer a different interpretation of the Holding Company Act. Rather than viewing the passage of holding-company regulation as an extension of New Deal restrictions, I see the act as signifying the first attempt, and victory, of those who would modify New Deal financial regulation. This is because although efforts at engineering holding-company regulation were conceived in a competitive-coalition setting, they evolved in a context typical of bank-dominant coalitions. As the subsystem context changed, so did the nature of regulation sought. In the end, although regulation was extended to a faction of the financial industry, it also provided an opening for the majority of banks to engage in activity previously prohibited by New Deal regulation.

The tale of holding-company regulation illustrates several important features of policymaking in a subsystem setting. First, although the holding-company case demonstrates the importance of shared beliefs in the formation of coalitions, it also illustrates the dynamic nature of beliefs. In the case of financial regulation this dynamism is linked primarily to economic variables. Policy learning occurs as a result of changes in the economic environment in which banks operate. Equally important, regulators often act as the principal idea entrepreneurs in the subsystem. As such, they are able to alter the content of regulatory policy if they can persuade legislators and the regulated to alter key tenets of their policy beliefs.

Second, coalition membership is an important determinant of whether policy change occurs. At least one of the principal financial-industry trade associations— either the IBAA or the ABA—had to be involved if serious discussion was to occur. More important, both had to agree for change to occur. Related to this, visible, active coalitions manifest themselves only when there is some dissonance within the subsystem. This dissonance is often, but not always, caused by events outside the subsystem realm of control. The most notable environmental variable involved the White House and FDR's regulatory efforts under the Second New Deal. In addition, changes in party control of Congress, alteration in the identity of the Banking Committee chair, World War II, and the end of the depression all contributed to alterations in subsystem politics and the nature of policy discourse.

BANK HOLDING COMPANIES: DEFINITION AND HISTORY

By law, bank holding companies include at least one chartered bank, the controlling interest of which is held by a single nonbank corporation. Banks that are part of multiple-bank holding companies can be distinguished from branches in that the various banking offices, although associated with a single corporate entity, are themselves legally distinct institutions. Holding companies are controversial because the parent company, the holding company, is often engaged in nonbanking activities. Thus holding-company arrangements allow banks to associate with firms involved in a wide variety of activity normally prohibited to commercial banks by New Deal regulation.

Holding companies have a long history in the world of banking. Holding company–like arrangements can be traced to the chain systems in New York in the 1820s and 1830s and the numerous state bank systems in the Midwest during the same period (Fischer 1961 and 1968; Lamb 1962; Wilburn 1967). Chains were formed when a group of banks decided to pool their assets so as to better weather fluctuations in demands for scarce resources, usually much-needed specie. In the rural setting chains were especially common among banks dealing in farm mortgages and agricultural loans, where there was a regular pattern of periods of slack and tight demand for currency. In urban areas banks active in the trust field often pooled resources so as to share the risk of investment in the securities markets.

In addition to risk-spreading, chain and group arrangements were also used by banks interested in getting around statutory prohibitions against expansion (Fischer 1968, 75). Central city banks in New York and Chicago used holding companies and chain arrangements to circumvent branching prohibitions and gain access to the lucrative savings bank business, which had developed in outlying districts.

Finally, some chains were simply exercises in speculation, with a group of investors using the stock of one bank as collateral to purchase other banks in a pyramid scheme of sorts. Such speculative activity was partially responsible for the widespread failure among banks during the panic of 1907 and gave rise to some of the first demands for the control, if not prohibition, of such activity (Fischer 1968, 77–78; Corey 1930, 254–262). Panics aside, by the 1930s holding companies were well established in the Upper Midwest and on the West Coast, with First Bankcorp in Minneapolis–Saint Paul and Transamerica in California the leading examples of the holding-company phenomenon. The major problem in regulating holding companies involved the preceding mix of activities and the rationales for organizing as a holding company. Although controlling speculation was the nominal target, any simple prohibition of holding-company arrangements would affect all practitioners.

The first concerted legislative effort to control the activities of bank holding companies was incorporated in the Banking Act of 1933. The New Deal financial regulation targeted the speculative use of holding companies. Yet it applied only to banks that were members of the Federal Reserve system, in effect making compliance voluntary, since nonmember banks were not compelled to join the system.[1] This legislative slip was a contributing factor in the formation of an industry trade association, the IBAA, which lobbied Congress for protection against "unfair" competition—most notably branching and holding-company arrangements.

Bills targeting bank holding companies were introduced in nearly every session of Congress following the passage of the Banking Act of 1933. Indeed, in the realm of financial regulation only branching attracted more attention from legislators over time (and in the mind of many the two were not distinct phenomena). Yet it was not until 1948 that either chamber reported a bank holding-company bill out of committee, and the actual passage of legislation did not occur for another eight years.

THE NEW DEAL REGULATORY ETHOS AND BANK HOLDING COMPANIES

Serious discussion of holding-company regulation began as a presidential project, introduced in Congress in 1938 as a part of Franklin Roosevelt's larger effort against public utility holding companies and oligopolistic business practices. Figure 6.1 summarizes the dynamics of policy formulation during this period. The continuing economic depression, highlighted by the sudden downturn in the economy in 1938 after a brief period of recovery, caused a renewed scrutiny of banking practices. Banks in particular merited only a few lines in the original presidential address, but they were singled out a few weeks later by Secretary of the Treasury Henry Morgenthau in testimony before the Senate Banking Committee. Holding companies were accused of threatening the very fiber of the newly created financial regulation.

Table 6.1 lays out the principal elements of the New Deal belief system enshrined in financial regulation. Notations in boldface are those the administration argued were threatened by holding-company arrangements. Most notable among the ideals threatened was the principle of preventing any undue concentration of economic power. By highlighting the threat posed to small (unit) banks by holding companies, the administration was actually referring to an ideal that predated the New Deal reforms. Advocates of unit banking argued that the

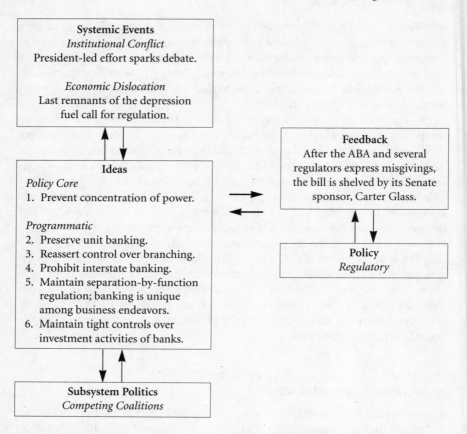

FIGURE 6.1   The dynamic of policy initiation: Glass-McAdoo, 1938

financial needs of citizens, business, and the polity were best served by local banks. They envisioned a system of small banks serving their local community as a bulwark against "moneyed interests" in New York City and elsewhere. Indeed, the OCC was charged in the original Bank Act of 1863 with chartering all qualified applicants in pursuit of this ideal.

Ironically, given the fear of centralized authority, the vehicle for accomplishing this end was a more powerful Federal Reserve. Holding-company regulation relaxed the prohibitions concerning the concentration of government power in order to diffuse economic power. Concentrating regulatory authority in the Federal Reserve altered the dual-banking system ideal, in which regulatory authority was split between national and state regulators, in favor of national regulators, since the Fed was to oversee state-chartered holding companies. It also altered the no-

TABLE 6.1   The New Deal Regulatory System Under Challenge

Policy Core	*Programmatic Incarnation*
Normative	
1. Industry should be preserved.	**1. Unit-banking ideal**
2. Consumers should be protected.	**2. Limited interstate banking**
3. Concentration of power is bad.	**3. No branching**
4. Markets are destructive.	**4. Investment restrictions**
5. Regulation is accomplished through management.	5. Consumers protected via regulatory prohibitions
6. Banking is distinct from other forms of business.	6. Deposit insurance
Empirical	7. Charter granting
1. Emphasize regulation; allow controlled competition.	8. Examinations
2. Dual regulation is divided between national and state authorities.	9. Regulation Q
3. Split regulation should be divided among OCC, Fed, FDIC, and FHLBB.	
4. Separation-by-function criteria apply.	

Note: **Boldface** indicates a belief is subject to challenge by a holding-company form of organization.

tion of split regulatory authority, a checks-and-balances system of regulation in which various national regulators shared policy responsibilities, in favor of the Federal Reserve.

Thus the solution to threats to the New Deal system were a series of reforms that in and of themselves altered the system. It was argued that this trade-off was necessary in order to preserve several additional programmatic elements—branching restrictions, investment prohibitions, separation-by-function criteria, and interstate banking prohibitions—essential to preserving unit banking and threatened by holding-company arrangements (see items 2 through 6 in Figure 6.1).

Following the executive-branch lead, Democratic members from both bank committees introduced legislation providing for the elimination of bank holding companies. The Senate version, the Glass-McAdoo bill, sought to "preserve the system of unit banking which was threatened by holding companies"; it became the administration vehicle of choice (*New York Times,* March 2, 1938). Interesting enough, two of the primary bank regulators—the OCC and the Fed—offered only halfhearted backing for the presidential initiative. Indeed, in contrast to the presidential call for the elimination of holding-company arrangements, their support was only for extending regulation so as to prevent an undue concentration of economic power and enforce select programmatic restrictions. The comptroller refused to endorse any plan that recommended the elimination of holding companies or ruled out their future expansion under any condition. The Fed actually published a study documenting a drop in the number and assets of bank holding companies—suggesting they were not the problem portrayed by the administration (*New York Times,* February 6, 1938). The position of the OCC and the Fed mirrored the feelings of much of the banking industry itself. Although the major industry trade association, the ABA, did not launch a full-scale attack on the holding-company bill, its silence on the issue was interpreted by many to be a ringing nonendorsement of the new legislation.

The inability of the administration to push its bill through the chamber can be traced to a number of factors. The original prohibitions contained in the 1933 reforms had been imposed on the financial subsystem during the crisis associated with the Great Depression. The passage of New Deal banking legislation was aided by the reluctant consensus among subsystem players that mismanagement, stock market speculation, and a loss of confidence were somehow connected to the problems of 1933. Although the economy was by no means out of the grip of the depression in 1938, the financial subsystem was no longer paralyzed by bank failures and interindustry conflict. Still smarting from the imposition of regulation by an outsider, many subsystem players—regulators and regulated—banded together to prevent a recurrence of the events of 1933 and 1935. Senate Banking Committee chair Carter Glass, displaying second thoughts on the wisdom of pursuing a course of action that caused dissonance within the financial subsystem, chose to shelve the administration bill (*New York Times,* May 4, 1938).

HOLDING COMPANY REGULATION:
FROM PROHIBITION TO MANAGEMENT, 1945–1956

The issue of holding-company regulation lay dormant during World War II, inching its way back onto the agenda following the cessation of hostilities. The postwar debate took on a decidedly different tone. Holding-company regulation was transformed from a strongly punitive instrument meant to discipline wayward members of the banking community into something more akin to a tool for managing banks experimenting with new organizational forms and investments.

Reintroduced in both chambers in 1947, holding-company regulation focused on delimiting the sort of activity that made a bank a holding company. It was an exercise, quite literally, to determine what constituted legitimate business activity by banks. Although the New Deal regulatory system had seemingly answered this question through the separation of commercial and investment banking, prohibitions against insurance underwriting, and the division of functions between thrifts and commercial banks, some subsystem players were not entirely pleased with the results. The attempt to modify the New Deal regulatory system can be explained by the shift in subsystem politics from competitive to bank-dominant, the role of Federal Reserve chair Marriner Eccles as policy entrepreneur, and the simmering discontent of many bankers.

Postwar efforts to pass holding-company regulation can be divided into four phases. The first involves the Tobey bill, introduced in 1947 and authored by Marriner Eccles of the Federal Reserve. As the first effort to actually define what sort of activity made a bank a holding company, the Tobey bill set the stage for all that followed. The second attempt to settle the definitional issue took the form of the Maybank-Robertson bill, a Senate-authored effort at regulating holding-company activities. The third phase, Capehart and Robertson, can be distinguished from its predecessors by the clear division of subsystem actors into distinct coalitions, each represented by its own legislative vehicle. The final phase culminated in the passage of the Bank Holding Company Act of 1956.

The Tobey Bill

The first piece of postwar holding-company legislation, the Tobey bill, was named after the newly installed Republican chair of the Senate Banking Committee, Charles W. Tobey. In addition to the change in party control of the Senate, the turnaround of the economy greatly influenced the course of policy debate in the financial subsystem (see Figure 6.2). The postwar economic boom eased outsiders out of the subsystem, although it did not eliminate the topic of holding-company regulation. Senator Tobey, a banker from New Hampshire, was concerned with the threat posed by holding companies to unit banking. Authored by Federal Reserve Board chair Marriner Eccles, a holding-company banker from Utah, the bill called for bank holding companies to divorce themselves from their nonbanking interests, submit to federal examination and regulation, and cease the practice of making "upstream" loans (loans to subsidiaries of the parent company) (*New York Times,* March 11, 1947). It defined holding companies as "any company which directly or indirectly owns, controls or holds with power to vote [fifteen] percentum or more of the voting shares of each of two or more banks" (U.S. Congress, Senate [hereafter Senate] 1947, 1). One-bank holding companies were exempted from the legislation unless they operated one or more branches, in which case they were treated the same as two-bank operations. The bill vested regulatory responsibility for enforcing the act in the Fed. It granted the Fed power to declare an operation a holding company even if it did not meet the preceding criteria, as well as the ability to exempt companies from regulation. Neither of the preceding broad grants of administrative discretion went unnoticed.

Several features distinguish the Tobey bill from earlier regulatory efforts (see "Ideas" in Figure 6.2). Perhaps most prominent was the lack of a provision for killing holding-company arrangements per se. Eccles was quite explicit on this point, arguing that holding companies that limited themselves to banking activities should not be outlawed, simply subjected to federal examination and regulation.[2]

94

```
┌─────────────────────────────────────┐
│            Systemic Events           │
│             Party Politics           │
│   Party control of Senate changes.   │
│                                      │
│          Economic Dislocation        │
│     Economic recovery is under way.  │
└─────────────────────────────────────┘
```

Ideas

Policy Core
1. Control concentration of power.   The prevention goal is relaxed in two ways: first, the Tobey bill calls for the regulation, not elimination, of holding companies; second, it places regulatory authority in the Fed, concentrating authority in a single national-level regulator and qualifying the dual and split regulation elements of the policy core.

Programmatic
2. Preserve unit banking.   Unit banking is modified in that one-bank holding companies are exempted from regulation.
3. Reassert control over branching.   This remains unchanged; banks with branches are considered holding companies.
4. Limit interstate banking.   The goal is changed from prohibiting to limiting through the creation of a one-bank loophole that allows some interstate banking, as well as increased investment activities, and a relaxation of the separation-by-function distinction for one-bank holding companies.
5. Maintain most separation-by-function regulation; banking is unique among business endeavors.   Two-bank holding companies must clearly separate their banking from nonbanking business.
6. Manage investment activities of banks. Two-bank holding companies must not engage in upstream loans.

Feedback
After the legislation is reported out of committee the ABA, state-level regulators, and the OCC oppose it, at which point it is dropped.

Policy
Regulatory and Distributive

Subsystem Politics
Bank-Dominant

FIGURE 6.2   The dynamic of policy formulation: The Tobey Bill, 1947

This was no minor point; it was insisted on by most regulators and much of the financial industry. A second important feature was the effort to offer an explicit definition of a holding company. The significance of this effort cannot be overemphasized. It marked the beginning of serious negotiation over just who would be subject to regulation and which interests would be exempted. It was also a debate over what types of activity were compatible with "safe and sound" banking. The emphasis of the debate shifted ever so subtly to a discussion of "reforming" the central principles of the New Deal regulatory regime, or at least making adjustments in some of the key ideas at the heart of New Deal regulation.

Holding-company regulation after Glass-McAdoo argued for the relaxation of one of the core tenets of the financial subsystem, the belief that regulation must guard against a concentration of power in both the public and private spheres. As institutionalized over time, the safeguard against a concentration of regulatory power took the form of regulatory responsibility shared between state and national regulators and at the national level, regulatory authority divided among the Office of the Comptroller, the Federal Reserve, and the Federal Deposit Insurance Corporation. By investing sole regulatory authority in a single national regulator—the Federal Reserve—the Tobey bill challenged these core beliefs.

Similarly, the safeguard against an undue concentration of economic power was challenged by the provisions exempting single-bank holding companies from regulation. This exemption favored those large banking interests inclined toward or already involved in such relationships. It also relaxed the programmatic beliefs regarding the near-sacred nature of unit banking, prohibitions on interstate banking, separation-by-function distinctions, and investment activities of banks (items 2 through 6 in Figure 6.2).

A major difference between the events of 1947 and those of 1938 was the primary role of the Fed as the author of holding-company legislation.[3] Much of the hearings during the 80th Congress were devoted to Fed chair Marriner Eccles's tutoring of the committee on the finer points of holding-company operations and the need to regulate the practice and expansion of such activity. Eccles argued that some holding companies were constructed simply as a device for getting around branching restrictions, federal examinations, and other regulations that ensured safe banking (Senate 1947). Eccles defined the problem in terms readily understandable to the legislators on the Banking Committee. Holding-company operations, if allowed to go unchecked, threatened local banks and the communities (read constituents) they served (Senate 1947; *New York Times,* May 27, 1947). Eccles was careful to cite the industry support he was able to marshal behind the legislation—portions of the Independent Bankers of America, a number of bank holding companies, the Association of Reserve City Bankers, and the Federal Advisory Council (twelve bankers from each of the twelve Federal Reserve districts selected by the various Reserve banks). Yet the Eccles-led coalition was more notable for those interests that were not members.

Soon after the Tobey bill was reported out of committee the ABA put together a well-orchestrated campaign against it. Openly allied with state regulators and with the tacit backing of the comptroller, it argued that the extension of Federal Reserve control over state nonmember banks threatened the dual-banking system itself (*New York Times,* June 3, 1947). In the end, the new holding-company legislation was never scheduled for floor debate and the Banking Committee let it die.

The events of the 80th Congress are important in that they were a *subsystem* affair. That is, executive branch influence was minimal. The definitional debate was dominated by subsystem regulars. Reporting the bill out of committee was simply the first salvo in what was to be a long and protracted campaign. The Tobey bill was one of the last gasps of the New Deal, at least when it came to bank regulation. Ironically, Senator Tobey, a New Hampshire Republican banker, was hardly a prototypical New Dealer.

Maybank-Robertson

Bank holding-company legislation was cosponsored in the 81st Congress (1949–1950) by the new chair of the Senate Banking Committee, Burnet R. Maybank, a South Carolina Democrat, and the chair of the Subcommittee on Federal Reserve Matters, A. Willis Robertson, a Democrat from Virginia. As Figure 6.3 illustrates, policy formulation during the 80th Congress occurred in a period of systemic quiescence. Although party control had shifted back to the Democrats in the Senate, this shift was hardly the stuff of ideological revolution. The economy was in the midst of a postwar boom, institutional rivalry was almost nonexistent following the earlier storm centered around the reelection of President Harry Truman, and the need for holding-company regulation seemed less important to both subsystem insiders and outsiders.

As was the case earlier, the debate centered around the definition of activity subject to regulation—quite simply, what constituted a holding company and what activities should be prohibited. Maybank-Robertson settled on the same two-bank definition contained in the Tobey bill, indicating that the policy was not driven by party affiliation. Single banks were exempted from regulation unless they operated four or more branches. In addition, the bill contained a section calling on the Fed to consider the opinion of state regulators when ruling on matters involving state banks and allowed the Fed to use state-, FDIC-, and OCC-administered exams in lieu of its own (Senate 1950, 12–14).

Thus Maybank-Robertson stuck with many of the changes proposed by Tobey (see Figure 6.3). There were, however, two major modifications proposed. The policy core concern with the concentration of regulatory authority was addressed through a provision that divided regulatory authority among state regulators, the Fed, FDIC, and OCC. Second, Maybank-Robertson actually loosened New Deal restrictions on branching by raising the number of branches allowed before a bank would fall under holding-company regulation.

Systemic Events
Party Politics
Party control of Senate changes.

Ideas
Policy Core
1. Control concentration of power. Control, rather than elimination, is now enshrined in all legislation dealing with holding-company operations. In addition, regulatory power is shared with state regulators when it comes to regulation of holding companies involving state-chartered institutions, and examination powers are shared with the FDIC and OCC.

Programmatic
2. Preserve unit banking.   The one-bank loophole is maintained.
3. Reassert control over branching. This is modified somewhat. Now only banks with four or more branches are considered holding companies.
4. Limit interstate banking.   The one-bank loophole is retained.
5. Maintain most separation-by-function regulation; banking is unique among business endeavors. Two-bank holding companies must clearly separate their banking from nonbanking business.
6. Manage investment activities of banks.   Two-bank holding companies must not engage in upstream loans.

Feedback
Opposition to the bill consists of several major holding companies; the ABA, the OCC, and some Banking Committee legislators who bristle at the concentration of authority vested in the Fed by the proposed legislation; and some Banking Committee legislators allied with state regulators who view the bill as a threat to the dual-banking system.

Policy
Distributive and Regulatory

Subsystem Politics
Bank-Dominant in Senate
Competitive in House

FIGURE 6.3   The dynamic of policy formulation: Maybank-Robertson, 1949

Despite the changes there was still plenty of discussion within the subsystem concerning the need for, or the proper structure of, holding-company regulation. Although coalitions were beginning to take form, the stance of a variety of interests vis-à-vis regulation was murky. Much of this had to do with the nature of the proposed legislation. On the one hand the act was interpreted as an attempt to extend New Deal safety and soundness principles to a particular class of actors— multiple-bank holding companies. As such it attracted a large following of small unit banks, legislators, and the Federal Reserve. Although many in this proto-coalition were disappointed by what they labeled a weak regulatory effort, they supported any effort to enforce New Deal provisions dealing with destructive competition.

On the other side of the issue was a mixed bag of folks who opposed the legislation under consideration for any of a variety of reasons. The most extreme camp consisted of some of the largest holding-company operations—the Morris Plan and Transamerica—that vehemently opposed any extension of regulation. Another faction, composed of the ABA, the OCC, and some Banking Committee members, expressed the fear that the bill granted the Fed too much administrative discretion. This group's objections focused on the language of the bill, in particular the portion of the bill that allowed the Fed to decide if "controlling influence" was exercised by a suspected holding company. The leader of this faction was the comptroller of the currency, Preston Delano. Delano viewed the Fed-authored bill as a blatant attempt to grab OCC turf. He suggested that bank holding-company activities be subject to split regulation by the FDIC (for state non-member banks), the Fed (for state member banks), and the OCC (for national banks) (Senate 1950, 368). The comptroller argued that the division of authority among the three national regulators would check abuse by any single regulator— a principle enshrined in the dual-banking system and the New Deal revisions. What went unsaid by Delano was that split regulation would also maintain the hold of the OCC over the single largest piece of regulatory turf—national banks.

Loosely allied with the OCC-ABA coalition was a faction whose concerns centered on the threat to the dual-banking system and the notion of states' rights. Adherents to this line of argument viewed the bill as a federal intrusion on matters best left to the states. Especially active in the House, this coalition of state bank supervisors, state-chartered institutions, and legislators suggested the legislation was a thinly veiled attempt by the Fed to bring all state banks under national regulation.

The lack of a clear subsystem consensus in support of the bill compelled one of the original cosponsors, Senate Banking Subcommittee chair Robertson, to introduce a substitute (Senate 1950, 294). Robertson's attempt to meet the objections of the various coalitions succeeded only in alienating the one agency that had originally backed the bill—the Federal Reserve—making regulator opposition unanimous. No further action was taken and the legislation died in committee.

Trolling for Consensus: Capehart and Robertson

After a two-year hiatus, the Senate Banking Committee once again took up the subject of bank holding-company regulation in 1953 during the 83rd Congress. As indicated in Figure 6.4, this round of formulation was characterized by two political changes on the macrosystem front. The change in presidential administration with the Republican Dwight Eisenhower at the helm, as well as GOP control of Congress, appear to be major "happenings." Yet their actual impact on the course of holding-company regulation appears to have been mitigated by the continuing economic boom.

The Senate Banking Committee, split along party lines, was unable to come to an agreement on the shape of legislation to be offered. Deadlocked, it decided to hold hearings on two measures in an attempt to rally support among subsystem players for one or the other. The major difference between the GOP offering, the Capehart bill, and its Democratic counterpart, the Robertson bill, had to do with the definition of a holding company. The GOP bill settled on a two-bank definition, and the Democrats insisted on a one-bank definition (see Figure 6.4). This was no minor difference. The two-bank definition was tantamount to government sanction of single-bank holding companies—and thus a qualification of New Deal prohibitions. Both bills split regulatory authority among the Fed, the OCC, and the FDIC. The GOP bill gave state regulators an active role in enforcement of regulation; the Democrats required only that national regulators consult with state regulators.

In arguing for the Robertson bill, the Fed warned against the creation of powerful banking conglomerates allowed to violate separation-of-function barriers erected by the New Deal. The OCC, in contrast, argued that holding companies added much needed stability to banking and leaned toward the Capehart measure. The ABA, reluctant to endorse either bill, voiced concern with the degree of administrative discretion vested in regulators by both bills. In addition, it sought exemptions for service-related activities engaged in by holding-company affiliates and decried the lack of a clear, precise, and limited definition of a holding company in either bill. In reality, both bills offered quite clear and precise definitions of a holding company. They simply did not offer the definition desired by the ABA.

In the end, as might be expected, the only consensus reached was that it was better to do nothing than to report either piece of legislation out of committee. Since the status quo was not seriously hurting the interests of any subsystem player, it was preferred to any change with unforeseen costs and consequences.

The Bank Holding Company Act of 1956

As Figure 6.5 illustrates, the Democrats regained control of the House and Senate during the 84th Congress. The change in party control coincided with a consensus among the various financial regulators that holding-company regulation was

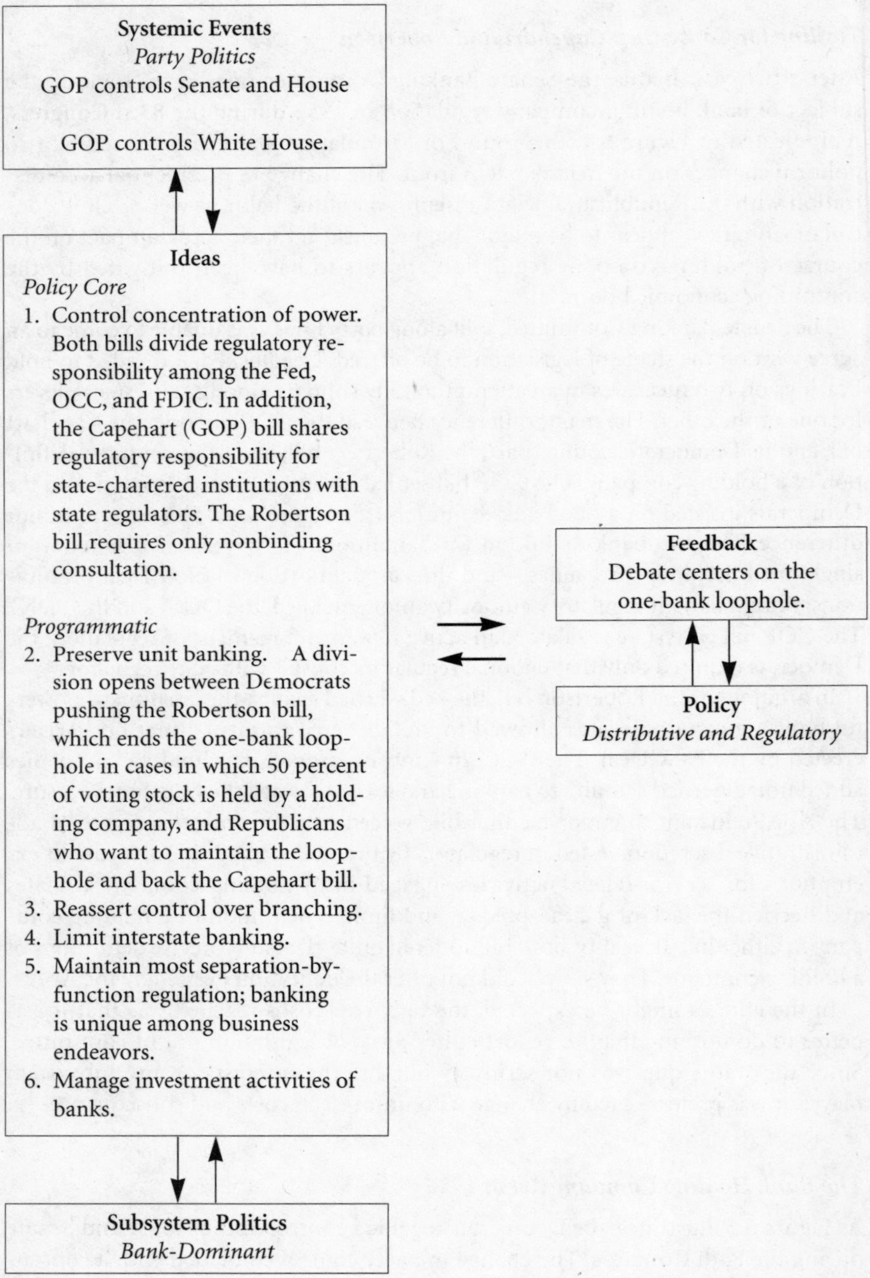

100

Systemic Events
Party Politics
GOP controls Senate and House

GOP controls White House.

Ideas
Policy Core
1. Control concentration of power.
   Both bills divide regulatory responsibility among the Fed,
   OCC, and FDIC. In addition,
   the Capehart (GOP) bill shares
   regulatory responsibility for
   state-chartered institutions with
   state regulators. The Robertson
   bill requires only nonbinding
   consultation.

Programmatic
2. Preserve unit banking.   A division opens between Democrats
   pushing the Robertson bill,
   which ends the one-bank loophole in cases in which 50 percent
   of voting stock is held by a holding company, and Republicans
   who want to maintain the loophole and back the Capehart bill.
3. Reassert control over branching.
4. Limit interstate banking.
5. Maintain most separation-by-
   function regulation; banking
   is unique among business
   endeavors.
6. Manage investment activities of
   banks.

Feedback
Debate centers on the
one-bank loophole.

Policy
Distributive and Regulatory

Subsystem Politics
Bank-Dominant

FIGURE 6.4   The dynamic of policy formulation: Capehart and Robertson, 1953

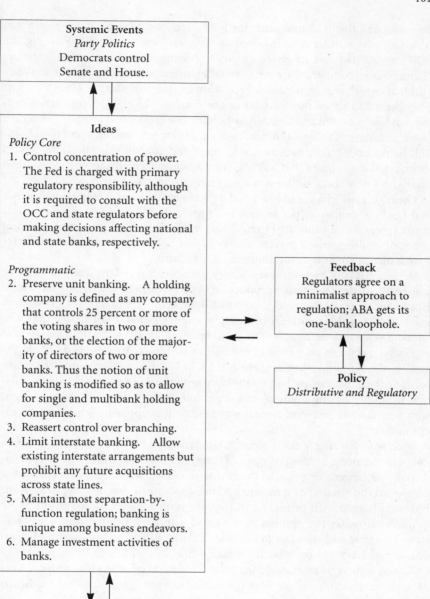

FIGURE 6.5   The dynamic of policy formulation: The Bank Holding Company Act of 1956

necessary and that it should cause the least disruption possible in the manner in which existing statutes were enforced. In an interesting bit of policy learning, the FDIC, which had first suggested an end to holding companies in 1937, argued, "Bank holding companies are not inherently dangerous nor do they, per se, create problems which require additional attention or scrutiny" (Senate 1955, 99). The Fed, which had staked out a similar position as far back as 1938, concurred, noting that banks owned and directed by holding companies had actually "presented fewer problems as to capital funds, asset condition, and management than ha[d] unit banks under independent management and control" (Senate 1955, 99). In short, regulators argued that holding-company arrangements were often more in tune with safety and soundness criteria than was unit banking.

The regulators' change of heart had a good deal to do with empirical evidence that holding companies per se were not unsafe. The lack of any significant systemic forces demanding strict regulatory enforcement—a president, political party, or well-organized private interests—led regulators to do what they preferred: manage their clients rather than police them.

Despite backing by several regulatory agencies, the system was still short of consensus, evident from the introduction of two rival pieces of legislation: a joint House-Senate effort that settled on a two-bank definition of a holding company; and a Fed-backed piece of legislation, sponsored by Senator Robertson, that contained a one-bank definition. The ABA, insisting on a one-bank loophole, also expressed a concern that none of the bills made it clear they applied only to the actions of holding companies (Senate 1955, 284–285). In other words, the major banking trade association had no problem with the extension of existing regulation to multiple bank holding companies but did not want regulators charged with a new, more stringent regulatory mandate that applied to the entire financial industry.

With ABA backing, a third piece of legislation, Robertson-Bricker, was introduced. It defined a holding company as any entity that controlled, directly or indirectly, 25 percent or more of the voting shares in two or more banks or that controlled the election of a majority of the directors of two or more banks. The Fed was charged with primary enforcement responsibility, although it was required to consider the opinion of the OCC with regard to national banks and state regulators and state law in the case of state banks. The acquisition of assets across state lines was prohibited unless specifically authorized by state law. The OCC and state regulators could file formal recommendations that proposed expansion be denied, in which case the Fed Board was required to hold a formal hearing, the findings of which were subject to judicial review.

The bill instructed the Fed to consider several features of any corporation filing a request to form a holding company, including its financial history and condition, its future prospects, the character of its management, local community needs, and the impact of the proposed action on the concentration of financial power in the area. This final provision was added in lieu of a suggestion that the

Justice Department Antitrust Division be included in the regulatory process, a move that regulators and regulated alike viewed as interference. Finally, the bill required the divestment of nonbanking interests within two years and the registration of all holding companies with the Fed.[4] The bill sailed through the Senate, passed in the House, and was signed into law as the Bank Holding Company Act of 1956.

TWO STEPS FORWARD AND ONE STEP BACK

Variation in subsystem politics clearly shaped holding-company regulation. The call for increased regulation was issued during a period of competitive politics when President Franklin Roosevelt took the opportunity to act as agenda setter. Subsystem politics are in turn affected by changes in the larger political-economic context. The first proposals for regulation were produced as part of the president-authored New Deal reforms, when the topic of economic regulation was still hot on the public agenda, the economy was still in the throes of the depression, and party control of the administration and Congress was in flux. Still, the real focus was on public utility holding companies. As time passed banking became less of an item on the public agenda, so by the time the holding-company regulation was passed it barely caused a ripple in the popular press.

The declining salience of banking policy, and holding-company regulation in particular, were linked to the decline of Democratic party dominance in the executive and legislature, economic recovery, and the fact that presidential attention was turned elsewhere. When events in the larger environment settled down, subsystem politics shifted back toward the bank-dominant equilibrium. The subsystem political shift corresponded with a change in the nature of the holding-company debate—from a focus on enforcement to a discussion of modification of New Deal regulatory tenets. Indeed, the consensus underlying the New Deal interpretation of safety and soundness principles unraveled when their presidential enforcer moved on to other pastures.

Most subsystem players exhibited little initial enthusiasm for additional presidential regulatory proposals coming out of the Roosevelt White House. Subsystem players—both banks and regulators—began to redefine the problem almost immediately and proved quite effective in preventing action on the issue until a mutually satisfying compromise was struck. Regulation was fashioned over the course of several sessions of Congress, during which regulators and the regulated dominated the discourse. As a result, the final legislative product was not nearly as stringent as the initial proposal. The parties involved settled on a distributive solution of economic opportunity under regulatory management rather than elimination of the holding-company form of organization. The inclusion of the one-bank loophole narrowed considerably the definition of activity subject to control, allowing the majority of the industry to engage in activity previously prohibited.

The process of formulating holding-company regulation illustrates the dynamics associated with subsystem political change. Still reeling from the shock of the depression and their inability to respond, banks and banking regulators were putty in the hands of a president intent on reining in powerful, and potentially destructive, holding companies. But typical of president-led coalitions, attention was soon focused on other matters.

A second major environmental shock—World War II—provided an environment in which subsystem regulars could resume control of financial regulation. The war not only diverted the attention of President Roosevelt, it provided a much needed boost to the economy and banking. This postwar economic and political environment proved less of a constraint to subsystem policymaking than the tumultuous period of the New Deal. Whereas the shift in party control of the Senate and House from Democrat to Republican and back again changed the leadership of the banking committees, it produced only a minor alteration in the course of subsystem policymaking. Indeed, postwar prosperity allowed subsystem players to regain control of policymaking.

Still, holding-company regulation remained alive because of a rift between banks over the possible abuse of the holding-company form of organization. Banks on the whole agreed that multibank giants like Transamerica were a threat. Yet not all were convinced that this innovation in organization was a bad thing per se. Thus, the majority of the banking industry managed to have itself exempted from the more punitive portions of the Bank Holding Company Act of 1956. The one-bank loophole and the provision acknowledging that the act applied only to multibank holding companies were insurance that most of the industry would remain unaffected by the regulation. Indeed, it was presented with a new set of investment opportunities with the passage of the act. Small unit banks that feared increased competition managed to secure prohibitions against uncontrolled interstate expansion as well as guidelines governing intrastate expansion that considered the impact of expansion on existing institutions. Thus the New Deal attempt to manage competition and control economic concentration was modified only slightly.

Finally, the shift from competitive to bank-dominant coalitions illustrates how subsystem equilibrium tends toward bank-dominant politics. Why this is so has a good deal to do with the institutional basis of subsystems—the congressional committee system and the role of regulators. Congress, and the committee system, are naturally predisposed toward the creation and maintenance of policy monopolies. In the realm of financial regulation, Banking Committee members dominate the policy process, majority-party members dominate committee activity, and the committee and subcommittee chairs play the most important roles among party members. In the Senate, committee members sponsored all eleven holding-company bills introduced between the 75th and 84th Congress, majority-party members sponsored nine of these, and chairs served as primary sponsors on four of the nine. Committee members sponsored eleven of the twelve bills introduced in the House, majority-party members introduced eight of the eleven, and chairs signed on to six of those eight.

Yet the autonomy of committee members and chairs in particular is context-bound. Committees work hand in hand with regulators. Regulators were important as architects of change. Federal Reserve chair Marriner Eccles was instrumental in getting the holding-company bill rolling. The FDIC and OCC were important sources of information and education for committee members. Regulators themselves appear to be more comfortable in the role of financial-industry managers than policemen. That is, they actively sought ways to allow banks to diversify their income opportunities while prudently managing depositor funds. This managerial prerogative required regulators to iron out differences among financial-industry factions and convince legislators of the fit between established policy core beliefs and new programmatic initiatives. Their ability to do so has a good deal to do with the staying power of subsystem-induced equilibrium. This equilibrium was sorely tested in the 1980s, as Chapter 7 illustrates.

Banking on Change: The Partial Deregulation of the Financial Industry

The partial deregulation of the financial industry in the 1980s is a textbook example of how exogenous events, policy learning, and sustained conflict can alter subsystem-induced equilibrium. Yet it is just as clearly a case that demonstrates the strength of subsystem arrangements. The partial deregulation of the financial industry was the product of subsystem politics in that it was largely orchestrated and controlled by the principal players—public and private—in the financial subsystem. Financial deregulation was also a part of a deregulatory wave that engulfed the larger political-economic system in the late 1970s and crested in the early 1980s. In short, the movement toward financial deregulation was part of a larger deregulatory "urge" whose ultimate form was mediated by the desires of public and private actors, institutional arrangements, and fundamental beliefs that lay at the heart of the financial subsystem.

In focusing on how the deregulatory ideal came to be adopted by a significant cohort of the financial subsystem, this study illustrates both the susceptibility of subsystems to outside forces and their resilience in the face of such challenge. Deregulation was not inevitable; rather it was chosen only after key players underwent a "deregulatory conversion" of sorts. The story of financial deregulation, although interesting in itself, presents a parable illustrating the dynamic of subsystem change. How the financial subsystem weathered the deregulatory era says a good deal about the durability and functioning of the wavering-equilibrium solution to the policy puzzle that is the American polity.

DEREGULATION COMES TO MAMMON:
DOING THE ECONOMIC TWO-STEP

Deregulation swept through the U.S. polity in the 1980s like a policy tidal wave. One set of astute observers likened deregulation to the latest policy fashion; all of Washington was sporting some version of it by the mid-1980s (Derthick and Quirk 1985). The deregulatory wave of the 1980s had roots in two separate, yet interrelated, urges—*administrative reform* and *regulatory policy change* (Eisner

1993, 170–171; Derthick and Quirk 1985, 29–35; Harris and Milkis 1989). *Administrative reform* focused on the administrative or managerial aspects of regulation and was principally a presidential project. "Reform" constituted an effort to rationalize the coordination of the various agencies charged with regulatory mandates. As such it brought the chief executive into direct conflict with Congress, since it often involved an attempt to exert executive influence over independent agencies. *Regulatory policy change*, the other side of deregulation, called for the elimination of "burdensome" and "unnecessary" regulation. It was a straightforward attempt to alter the course of regulatory policy that began as a project dominated by economists but soon expanded its following to include a wide variety of subsystem players.

Both administrative reform and policy change were a direct assault on the variety of beliefs institutionalized in the New Deal regulatory setup. The New Deal, building on beliefs enshrined in the Bank Acts of 1863 and 1865 as well as the Federal Reserve Act, created a system of regulation that emphasized safety of depositors' funds and the soundness of financial intermediaries. Table 7.1 documents the belief system that served as the basis of these institutional arrangements. Among the normative elements of the policy core beliefs are those dating from the founding of the banking system, such as equity of service and fear of

TABLE 7.1   The New Deal Regulatory Belief System (as enshrined in regulation)

Policy Core	*Programmatic Incarnation*
Normative	
1. **Industry should be preserved.**	1. **Regulation Q**
2. **Consumers should be protected.**	2. **Limit interstate banking**
3. **Concentration of power is bad (unit-banking ideal).**	3. **No branching**
	4. **Investment restrictions**
4. **Markets are destructive.**	5. **Protect consumers via regulatory prohibitions**
5. Regulation is accomplished through management.	
	6. Deposit insurance
6. **Banking is distinct from other forms of business.**	7. Charter granting
	8. Examinations
Empirical	
1. Emphasize regulation; allow controlled competition.	
2. Dual regulation is divided between national and state authorities.	
3. **Split regulation is divided among OCC, Fed, FDIC, and FHLBB.**	
4. **Separation-by-function criteria.**	

Note: **Boldface** indicates a belief is subject to challenge by a suggested change in financial regulation arising out of the deregulatory debate.

concentration of power, as well as those unique to the New Deal, such as regulation as risk management and the belief that markets are destructive (for a more complete discussion of these see Chapter 2). Empirically based policy core elements include the goals of preserving the financial industry (dating at least as far back as the Federal Reserve Act), consumer protection, dual and split regulation, and controlled competition. These policy core beliefs were given life vis-à-vis a variety of programmatic incarnations, also listed in Table 7.1.

The story of financial deregulation can be divided into five phases. During the first (1973–1974), a period characterized by bank-dominant politics in the House and transitory coalitions in the Senate, the president-sponsored Hunt Commission served as a vehicle for advocates of deregulation in the Senate. Led by a Republican president and orchestrated by economists, the Hunt Commission was the first overt, concerted challenge to New Deal programmatic and policy core beliefs since the passage of regulatory legislation in the 1930s.

The House-sponsored *Financial Institutions and the Nation's Economy (FINE)* study, 1975, marks the beginning of the second phase of deregulatory politics. *FINE* was engineered by House Banking Committee Democrats during a period characterized by competitive coalitions. Uncertainty as to the actual source of the problems plaguing the economy, as well as the outcome of pursuing a deregulatory solution, led to policy stalemate.

The third phase, culminating in 1980, is marked by the worsening of economic circumstances, technological changes in banking, and a shift in party control of the White House. This phase ends with the passage of the Depository Institutions Deregulatory and Monetary Control Act of 1980 (DIDMCA). Because of the activities of outsiders allied with subsystem insiders, DIDMCA actually served to curtail the extent of financial deregulation.

The fourth phase, 1980–1982, marked by the enactment of Garn–St. Germain, is best characterized as institutionalized stalemate rather than any clear exercise of authority. The lack of a definitive resolution to the problems plaguing banking was due in part to their nature—an increasing number of financial-institution failures—and uncertainty about how to best deal with them. It can also be attributed to the institutional stalemate produced by the differing philosophies of the chairs of House and Senate Banking Committees and the competitive coalitions that dominated the subsystem.

The final act of the deregulatory drama, 1982–1990, opened with the disintegration of the savings and loan insurance fund and a sizable portion of the thrift industry with it. It closed with regulator-sponsored deregulation that provided increased earning opportunities, and risk, for surviving thrifts and commercial banks. What did not occur in the financial realm was complete deregulation. Rather, a sort of institutionalized stalemate greeted the 1990s. Why this was so can be explained, at least in part, by the persistence and longevity of subsystem arrangements and the ideas that support them. I now turn to that story.

TROUBLE IN PARADISE:
THE HUNT COMMISSION AND REGULATORY REFORM

There was a sprinkling of calls for regulatory reform in the decades following the construction of the New Deal financial regulatory system, but none attracted sustained, serious attention until 1973. In that year the topic was reintroduced as part of President Nixon's Commission on Financial Structure and Regulation, or as it is more commonly known, the Hunt Commission. The Hunt Commission attacked the New Deal–based system of financial regulation as inefficient. It offered a solution of limited regulation—eliminating many of the statutory distinctions separating commercial banks, thrifts, and investment banking (the so-called separation-by-function criteria)—to be carried out by reformed regulatory institutions.

A reaction to the changing economic climate of the 1970s, and the slowdown in housing starts in particular, the Hunt Commission brought in economists to explain the seemingly unexplainable economic performance of the early 1970s (see Figure 7.1). Banking issues were gaining in salience because the New Deal regulatory setup seemed unable to solve the problem of increasingly tight credit. Launching a frontal assault on the policy core and programmatic beliefs enshrined in the New Deal belief system, economists argued that financial institutions had been "massively over-regulated since the 1930's" (U.S. Congress, House [hereafter House] 1973b, 259). That is, regulation was the problem, not the solution. The economists' challenge jarred the ideational equilibrium in the financial subsystem, beginning a process of alignment and realignment that would occupy the next decade.

During the initial division in the subsystem, bank regulators, joined by the leading banking trade group, the American Bankers Association (ABA), pushed for the relaxation of select New Deal regulatory restrictions. They were joined in their cause by a senior member of the Senate Banking Committee—William Proxmire (Democrat from Wisconsin)— academic economists, and the Nixon White House. Although united on deregulation, the regulatory members of the coalition parted ways with the White House on the question of redistributing regulatory responsibilities and reorganizing regulatory agencies.

In the opposition camp were the trade association representing smaller banks (the Independent Bankers Association of America [IBAA]), both thrift trade associations (the United States Savings and Loan Association [USSLA] and the National League of Insured Savings Associations [NLISA]), and most Banking Committee members. Indeed, members of the Democrat-controlled Senate Banking Committee were more interested in the relationship between the Republican president and several of the regulators that backed change—the OCC, FDIC, and FHLBB—than in the actual proposals for change in the regulatory system. Banking Committee legislators expressed alarm with the procedures followed by the Hunt Commission: closed meetings, no public input, little in the way of consultation with regulators, and domination by individuals representing

Systemic Events
Institutional Conflict
White House pursues an administrative
presidency strategy. The Hunt Commission
provides an opening in the Senate.

Economic Dislocation
Housing starts to drop due to a
tightening of credit.

Ideas
Policy Core
1. Split regulation is challenged by economists on efficiency grounds.
2. Dual regulation is challenged by advocates of universal Fed membership.
3. The notion that banking is distinct from
   other forms of business is implicitly challenged by the Hunt report.

Programmatic
4. Remove Regulation Q.
5. Relax separation-of-function criteria.
   This involves several proposals that include eliminating preferential tax treatment of thrifts, allowing securities underwriting, broadening thrift commercial
   lending powers, and relaxing real estate
   loan restrictions applying to commercial
   banks.

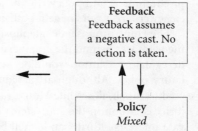

Feedback
Feedback assumes
a negative cast. No
action is taken.

Policy
Mixed

Subsystem Politics
Economists are important idea entrepreneurs. House politics are bank-dominant
and the Senate's are transitory. Coalitions engaged in competition include an antichange
coalition consisting of Bank Committee
members, thrifts, the FHLBB, and the IBA
and a presidential, economist, regulator, and
ABA coalition.

FIGURE 7.1   The dynamic of subsystem change: The Hunt Commission, 1973

the larger players in the financial industry. In the view of these legislators, regulators were being duped by the administration and large banks.

Clearly, the majority of Banking Committee members viewed the Hunt proposals as interference in subsystem business. If this institutionally based suspicion was not enough, committee member fears of the political risks associated with deregulation tipped the scales against action. The Senate committee in particular focused on the impact deregulation would have on mortgage markets, home starts, and consumers as mortgage borrowers. In the end, even the regulators who backed some form of deregulation had to admit it was impossible to predict with any certainty the actual outcome of regulatory change. Federal Reserve Board governor Robert Holland acknowledged they were moving into uncharted territory, suggesting Fed economists "believe it would be stretching their analytical devices beyond the area where they could be helpful" in attempting to predict the consequences of deregulation (U.S. Congress, Senate [hereafter Senate] 1973b, 157–161). Similarly, the FDIC chair allowed that some of the proposals for change entered "an area of the unknown" (Senate 1973b, 402). Still, regulators appeared more willing to alter programmatic and policy core beliefs, arguing that gradual change based on efficiency criteria would benefit both consumers and financial institutions.

The Hunt-proposal debate illustrates how uncertainty—in this case determining what was behind the credit crunch in housing as well as what the costs of the deregulatory solution would be—can inhibit attempts to alter the course of regulatory policy. Although attracted to financial regulation by the salience of the credit crunch, the White House ran into problems when it failed to build a majority coalition in the subsystem. The largest source of resistance was from private interests—thrifts and small banks and associated businesses such as home builders. In addition, institutional tension between the executive and the Senate and House Banking Committees stymied White House efforts to alter institutional arrangements. Finally, although material self-interest was clearly driving the private interests involved in the deregulatory debate, regulators and some legislators appeared more interested in simply making good policy. As such, they were not convinced that the efficiency criteria being pushed by economists should replace the safety and soundness principles of the New Deal policy core.

ROUND TWO: THE *FINE* STUDY

If the Hunt proposals were a president-led attempt to alter subsystem arrangements, the 1975 *FINE* study was the House Banking Committee effort to reassert control. Commissioned by the House Banking Committee with the intention of bringing its members up to speed on the changing environment of banking, the *FINE* study illustrates how environmental factors can provoke reevaluation of institutional arrangements and the ideas behind them (see Figure 7.2). This reevaluation, it should be added, involved not just subsystem insiders but outsiders as well.

Systemic Events
Economic Dislocation
Several high-profile bank failures.

Consumer-savers demand greater
return on their investment.

Mortgage borrowers are hurt by a
return to a tight mortgage market.

Ideas
Policy Core
1. The notion that banking is distinct
   from other forms of business is again
   subject to challenge.
2. Split regulation is challenged by *FINE*
   and the Federal Reserve on efficiency
   grounds, although the Fed later aban-
   dons the attempt to consolidate regulator responsibilities in a single
   agency.

Programmatic
3. Remove Regulation Q.
4. Relax separation-of-function criteria.
   This involves several proposals that
   include eliminating preferential tax
   treatment of thrifts, allowing securities underwriting, broadening thrift
   commercial lending powers, and relaxing real estate loan restrictions applying to commercial banks.

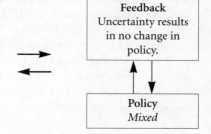

Feedback
Uncertainty results
in no change in
policy.

Policy
Mixed

Subsystem Politics
Competitive in the Senate, with the financial industry fracturing and no other
potential coalition coming to the fore.
In the House a competing coalition of
consumers dominates the debate. The
financial industry splinters into pro- and
antichange coalitions.

FIGURE 7.2   The dynamic of subsystem change: The *FINE* Study, 1975

Three economic problems in particular attracted a good deal of attention. The first involved several notable bank failures due to fraud. Any bank failure sets off alarm bells on the banking committees; these failures were particularly troublesome because they went unnoticed due to poor communications and a lack of coordination among OCC examiners, the Fed, and FDIC personnel. This interagency communications failure made the Hunt and *FINE* arguments for administrative reform resonate on the banking committees. Even financial regulators recognized that it was increasingly difficult to regulate or manage their industry clients in the changing environment of the 1970s.

A key feature of the changing economic environment of the 1970s was inflation, a problem that hit thrifts particularly hard. Remember, a key distinction between thrifts and commercial banks is their customer base. Thrifts are primarily engaged in long-term mortgage lending, and banks are concerned with short-term commercial lending. By the 1970s this difference in customer base left thrifts with portfolios of mortgages that produced below-market rates of return due to low interest rates on long-term mortgages and the inflationary spiral engulfing the economy. Commercial banks were similarly hurt; however, their loan portfolios tended to mature much faster, so they were not as locked into losing investments as were their thrift cousins. New Deal regulation prevented financial intermediaries from raising interest rates to keep pace with the market. The result was that thrifts were reluctant to make mortgage loans at artificially low fixed rates of interest, which would actually cost them money in the long run. Mortgage borrowers, home builders, and real estate agents suffered because of the slowdown in lending, home starts, and sales.

In addition to losing income on existing mortgages and loans, neither thrifts nor banks were able to attract new depositors or keep old ones because neither was able to match the return promised by other forms of investment—stocks and banklike stock instruments (Meier 1985). Quite simply, consumers-as-savers were no longer well served by the system of fixed interest rates. The fact that savers could realize a greater return on their investment elsewhere led to the increased loss of deposits in all forms of financial intermediaries, or to what is known as disintermediation (Cargill and Garcia 1985). All three of these economic quandaries provided a potential opening for advocates of policy change. At the same time they also provided a basis for resisting radical change.

Altering Institutional Arrangements

The *FINE* discussion principles, much like the Hunt report, called for both policy change and administrative reform. The *FINE* authors quoted approvingly a 1974 speech by Fed chair Arthur Burns in which Burns characterized the regulatory setup as "a jurisdictional tangle that boggles the mind" (House 1975b, 11). The Fed chair argued that split regulation fostered "competition in laxity," in which regulators created as lax a regulatory environment as possible so as to curry favor with the regulated industry. Burns's criticism was aimed at the comptroller, the Fed's major rival in the regulation of commercial banking. The OCC had approved a variety of banking practices deemed unsound by the Fed. Burns apparently viewed *FINE* as an opportunity to rein in the OCC and establish Fed preeminence in financial regulation. Thus he backed modification of core policy principles dealing with split regulatory authority in an effort to shore up safety and soundness principles.

Despite the recognition by financial regulators of administrative problems built into the regulatory system, most opposed tinkering with the system, let alone radically restructuring it. Parting ways with the *FINE* authors, the FDIC, after weighing the arguments for and against consolidation, came out for the "controlled competition" of the existing system. The OCC took much the same stance, arguing that multiple agencies produced "competition in improvement" rather than "competition in laxity." Appealing to policy core beliefs regarding the centralization of power, the OCC chair argued that the regulatory system was deliberately designed as a system of checks and balances. Even the Fed backed off from its support of reform when the *FINE* authors recommended that Federal Reserve policy responsibilities be curtailed to include monetary questions only.

Focusing on the dangers inherent in the proposed concentration of regulatory power, the regulated industries made their case against institutional reform. The ABA worried that the *FINE*-envisioned reorganization violated the principles of dual banking and undermined the independence of the Federal Reserve. Echoing the ABA criticism, the IBAA suggested increased congressional oversight as the solution to jurisdictional disputes among federal regulators. The National Savings and Loan League (NSLL) argued against consolidation on the grounds that it would decrease efficiency rather than increase it, and the United States League of Savings Associations repeated the ABA contention that consolidation threatened the existence of the dual-banking system (House 1975b, 1489, 1507–1509, 1656–1657, 1696). In short, when it came to the question of regulatory reform, subsystem members were loath to alter, let alone abandon, policy core elements of the New Deal system. The case of deregulation was another matter. When the debate turned to loosening programmatic restrictions, the subsystem consensus became fractured.

Programmatic Change: Let the Games Begin

The debate over programmatic change solidified the fissures first apparent following the publication of the Hunt report. The division into two coalitions became clearer with a shift in membership and a hardening of the lines first delimited by the Hunt proposals. After the publication of *FINE,* a coalition of banking regulators, the chair of the House Banking Committee, and the ABA called for the relaxation of many of the programmatic elements of the New Deal system that distinguished thrifts from commercial banks. The interest-rate differential enshrined in Regulation Q came under intense scrutiny. Regulation Q allowed thrifts to offer a nominally higher rate of interest on savings than offered by commercial banks as a "reward" for making mortgage loans. Banks argued the differential was unnecessary and unfair and, if eliminated, would have little effect on the lucrative mortgage market as long as the cap on interest rates was also removed. The ABA argued the market, not regulation, should determine the interest rate paid depositors and charged borrowers.

Opposing the call for policy change were the thrift regulator, the Federal Home Loan Bank Board (FHLBB); the chair of the House Subcommittee on Financial Institutions, Fernand St. Germain (Democrat from Rhode Island); the savings and loan trade associations, the USLSA and the NSLL; the National Association of Home Builders; and small banks represented by the IBAA. Although there was some consensus among these actors that events in the larger environment were at the heart of the industry's problems—all the depository trade associations cited inflation and fiscal policy as primary causes of their woes, as did the Fed and FHLBB—there was no such consensus on the solution. Relaxing New Deal prohibitions was portrayed as opening the system to destructive competition reminiscent of depression-era banking.

The *FINE* case illustrates how systemic variables—economic change and institutional rivalry between the executive and legislature—affect the belief system of subsystem coalitions. As *FINE* demonstrates, elements of these belief systems are under constant stress. Although policy core beliefs move the system toward some type of equilibrium, the near-constant shifting of programmatic beliefs—caused in part by change in exogenous variables—moves the system toward disequilibrium. Disequilibrium—that is, the multiple and conflicting values and preferences held by politicians, bureaucrats, academics, and private interest groups—often leads to policy stalemate, dooming any attempt to exercise influence to a series of protracted conflicts.

In the case of regulatory reform, regulators proved loath to give up administrative responsibilities to fellow regulators. Such reluctance probably had something to do with the nature of bureaucratic organizations—organizational maintenance is a major imperative of all such arrangements—but it also reflected the different regulatory visions of the various regulators. The OCC viewed its mission in managerial terms; the FDIC tended to assume a consumer- or depositor-protection ethos. This meant the former was willing to allow banks some leeway in investments and the latter was much more conservative in carrying out examinations. Similarly, the Fed was more system-oriented, linking safety and soundness to issues regarding the conduct of monetary policy, and the goal of thrift regulators was to keep funds flowing for mortgages and ensure thrifts a fair return on same. Thus those interested in influencing policy were forced to search for some common ideational ground. This search became increasingly difficult as events unfolded and prevented any single actor from assuming the role of entrepreneur.

A major obstacle to adoption of deregulation was that even those who backed deregulation were uncertain as to the outcome of relying on "market discipline" to allocate credit. The uncertainty of the outcome associated with deregulation worried legislators, regulators, the regulated, and a host of folks associated with real estate and home building. Although economists attempted to settle nerves with rosy econometric forecasts, most subsystem players were still not buying. As the *FINE* case makes plain, when faced with uncertainty most legislators are reluctant to alter subsystem arrangements. In the end, although a deregulatory urge was beginning to surface in the larger environment and the financial subsystem, other concerns came to dominate the congressional agenda. *FINE* coincided with a major piece of tax-reform legislation and the more salient issue of the proposed bailout of New York City. When the mortgage market appeared to make a comeback, the issue of reform became much less important to outsiders, the financial industry, legislators, and regulators and was allowed to fade into temporary policy oblivion.

REGULATOR-SPONSORED DEREGULATION: THE ROAD TO THE DEPOSITORY INSTITUTIONS DEREGULATION AND MONETARY CONTROL ACT OF 1980

If changes in external conditions allowed subsystem actors to put off the question of regulatory change during the *FINE* hearings, events in the larger environment—principally changes in technology and inflation—worked with changes in banking itself to force reconsideration of reform proposals by 1979 (see Figure 7.3). Among the more noteworthy changes in banking technology were the development of electronic fund transfers (EFTs) and automated teller machines (ATMs). EFTs were commonplace in the securities industry by the time banking adopted the technology (White 1980). What EFTs did was allow the crediting or debiting of an account without the actual physical transfer of funds and accompanying paperwork (Bequai 1981). EFTs required banks to adopt the new computerized technology in dealing with customers and in their own internal operations.

ATMs were an outgrowth of the electronic revolution in banking. They allow customers to use a bank card to receive cash, make deposits, pay loans, and engage in a variety of banking business without ever setting foot in the bank. They are also a means of circumventing branching restrictions, since technically they are not branches.

The electronic revolution in banking—internal computerization, EFTs, and ATMs—allowed both banks and their customers to minimize their working balances and seek higher rates of returns on their money. The money market was transformed from a loose collection of regional entities to an international institution in the space of a decade (Colton and Kraemer 1980). Depositors became

Systemic Events
Economic Dislocation
Inflation exacerbates disintermediation (the loss
of depositor funds to investments that offer a
higher rate of return).

Changing technology in the form of electronic
fund transfers, ATMs, and innovations such as
NOW accounts makes much of regulation
inapplicable.

Institutional Conflict
The appeals court finds itself mediating a dispute
among financial intermediaries.

President Carter is riding a deregulatory wave, a
wave that crests as part of Reagan's administrative
strategy.

Ideas
Policy Core
1. The notion that banking is distinct from other
   forms of business is questioned.
2. The dual-banking principle is weakened through
   the provision requiring all insured banking institutions to join the Federal Reserve system.
3. Separation-by-function criteria are relaxed.

Programmatic
4. Regulation Q is subject to phaseout.
5. Interest on checking is provided through NOW
   accounts.
6. Thrifts are allowed to make commercial loans.
7. Banks are allowed to expand their real estate
   lending portfolios.
8. Thrifts are allowed three branches in the form
   of remote ATMs.

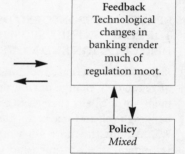

Feedback
Technological
changes in
banking render
much of
regulation moot.

Policy
Mixed

Subsystem Politics
A bank-dominant coalition controls the Senate; in
the House, competitive coalitions battle, for example, those made up of "nonbank banks" loosely allied with thrifts, the FHLBB, and the IBAA compete with national bank regulators and the ABA.

FIGURE 7.3   The dynamic of subsystem change: DIDMCA, 1980

more comfortable with moving their savings out of banks and thrifts and into instruments offering higher returns and banklike services.

In addition, a marketing innovation, the negotiable order of withdrawal (NOW) account, which provided checking-like services and paid interest, proved highly popular with customers. Invented by mutual savings banks and picked up by credit unions, NOW accounts began to attract more and more customers away from thrifts and banks as the decade progressed (Mayer 1974).

The new economic reality produced a shift in the debate concerning deregulation. Earlier arguments turned on the question of maintaining or altering specialization as enshrined in New Deal regulation, principally as it affected the mortgage market. In 1979 the debate over separation-by-function principles was expanded to include a discussion of the unique nature of depository institutions in general and of whether banking was really different from other forms of commerce. Debate now challenged not only programmatic elements of the New Deal belief system—indeed, many did not apply given technological changes under way—but also questioned many of the policy core elements that lay at the heart of financial regulation and beliefs about banking.

The issue was brought to a head when the U.S. Court of Appeals for the District of Columbia struck down regulator-approved innovations that blurred the distinction between types of financial intermediaries. The court issued a ruling upholding elements of the New Deal policy core, arguing that in pursuing administrative deregulation regulators had made "separate and distinct types of financial institutions . . . virtually identical . . . all without the benefit of congressional consideration and statutory enactment" (Conte 1979, 1365). The involvement of the appeals court was the result of several suits filed by the various financial-industry trade associations—the IBAA, ABA, CUNA (Credit Union National Association), and the USLSA—against the principal regulators of their industry rivals. Each association believed it was losing ground to the others as a result of regulator-authored change. Ironically, each sought to widen the scope of the conflict by enlisting the court as an ally. The end result was that the appeals court returned the ball to the Banking Committee court.

The appeals court delayed the enforcement of its judgment pending congressional action by January 1, 1980. The court's attempt to force congressional action coincided with the announcement from the White House of its own deregulatory agenda. The effort of the court aside, the House and Senate deadlocked, agreeing to a temporary measure that extended the practices challenged in the court suit for ninety days. The eventual result of the House-Senate impasse was the Depository Institutions Deregulation and Monetary Control Act of 1980 (DIDMCA).

Although usually cited as one of two legislative acts leading to deregulation, DIDMCA simply ratified what regulators had already wrought. The act contained two interrelated parts. New to the financial regulation scene was the monetary-control component, which increased Fed control over the money supply through the imposition of reserve requirements and other federal regulations on nonmember banks and nonbank depository institutions. The deregulatory portion removed or modified several New Deal regulations, many of which the various regulators had been bending for some time (Cargill and Garcia 1985). It phased out interest-rate ceilings for both thrifts and banks; authorized NOW accounts (essentially limited checking with interest) for all institutions; allowed insured banks to offer automatic transfer service, which permitted transfers from savings to checking accounts under select conditions; raised deposit insurance from $40,000 per account to $100,000; authorized remote-service units, which acted as quasi-branches, for thrifts; and loosened percent-of-asset restrictions on a wide variety of loans made by thrifts while also expanding the types of loans allowed thrifts.

Thus DIDMCA was like one of those signs that informs travelers they have just left a particular locale with no indication of their ultimate destination. It clearly prevented wholesale abandonment of the separation-by-function regulations of the New Deal system, yet it by no means turned the clock back on regulators' decisions to relax some of the New Deal prohibitions. It could not do so because regulators were backed by powerful clientele who insisted on pressing forward, and events themselves provided an environment conducive to change.

What is fascinating about DIDMCA is it seems to confound much of conventional theory regarding subsystems politics and the role of outsiders in particular. Although the financial industry was clearly divided by the deregulation question, it was outsiders who both pushed for a resolution and were instrumental in ensuring that one was not forthcoming. Consumers' demands resembled the "push me–pull you" phenomenon discovered by Doctor Dolittle. That is, while one faction argued for a better return on savings, another insisted on low-interest mortgages. Banking Committee legislators, caught in the middle, split on the best course of action for fear of alienating powerful constituents no matter what they did. Related to this, securities firms, insurance corporations, and the variety of nonbank banks engaged in banklike activities fought tooth and nail to curtail the extension of banking regulation to their enterprises while insisting it be maintained in banking.

The inability to agree on a common course of action played into the hands of those favoring the new status quo. Although nobody picked the new status quo as the ideal, it was the second choice of almost all involved. Deregulators preferred it to a return to the old system, and antichange forces preferred it to complete deregulation. Thus stalemate created a tenuous equilibrium much akin to Bosso's (1987) "presence politics." Outsiders ranging from consumers to securities and insurance firms fought to establish and maintain their presence in the financial subsystem in hopes of influencing the course of policy in future rounds.

FIDDLING WHILE ROME BURNS:
GARN–ST. GERMAIN

A good deal of the motivation behind DIDMCA was the belief that the problem facing the financial industry was overly restrictive regulation. The solution enshrined in DIDMCA, marking a shift from the New Deal reforms, was the removal of many of the regulatory restrictions and a return to a limited form of "market discipline." The problem with the DIDMCA solution was that it was untested, ran against many of the core policy beliefs of members of the financial subsystem, and in the end had very little effect on the disintermediation affecting the savings and loan industry.

The problems associated with implementing DIDMCA illustrate the chaos created by extra-subsystem events and subsystem members' inability to deal with the changing economic and political environment. Ironically, the Depository Institutions Deregulation Committee (DIDC), created by DIDMCA to oversee the gradual elimination of interest-rate ceilings, served as the principal means of preventing deregulation. DIDC was an institution charged with a new policy mandate but staffed with individuals who clung to old beliefs. Time and again the counsel split four to one against raising rates, with only the FDIC voting consistently for deregulation. DIDC viewed its primary role as preventing the collapse of the thrift industry, something its members feared would result if interest rates were raised at all during the early 1980s.

The problems of thrifts, and for that matter commercial banks, which were also undergoing a disintermediation crisis of their own, seemed to demand action in 1981, but little in the way of legislative relief was forthcoming. The inactivity can be explained by the leadership change on both banking committees, the change from Democrat to Republican party control in the Senate, and the alteration in policy beliefs concerning the proper form and role of financial regulation. The events surrounding Garn–St. Germain demonstrate how systemic events affect subsystem arrangements and the difficulty of policymaking under competitive coalitions (see Figure 7.4). In this case the battle involved a struggle in which congressional players figured prominently. The battle over the future course of financial regulation pitted the newly installed chairs of the Senate and House Banking Committees—Republican Jake Garn of Utah and Democrat Fernand St. Germain of Rhode Island, respectively—against one another. Garn's thinking on banking was a collection of mixed goals. He argued for dismantling much of financial regulation while favoring separation-by-function principles as essential to home financing (Gregg 1980a). Garn's slow conversion to deregulation while clinging to elements of New Deal regulatory principles was typical of the experience of a variety of subsystem players. In contrast, his House counterpart, Fernand St. Germain, was an adamant foe of deregulation. Allied with the FHLBB and backed by the thrift industry, home builders, and the IBAA, St. Germain was able to stymie any attempt to alter the course of policy despite the deregulatory mood in Washington and the nation (Gregg 1979b).

All this changed by late 1981, when it was clear that many thrifts were in a perilous condition. Squeezed between the demand for higher rates of return on savings and below-market-rate mortgages, more and more thrifts were showing up on the FHLBB's list of problem institutions. As the thrift insurance fund approached insolvency, the solvent, larger thrifts began to defect from the coalition.

Systemic Events
Economic Dislocation
Disintermediation is reaching crisis levels in both the thrift and banking industries.

Thrifts are failing in record numbers, bankrupting the FHLBB.

Party Politics
Republicans take control of the Senate. Jake Garn is the new Banking Committee chair.

Institutional Conflict
President Reagan continues to pursue deregulation.

Fernand St. Germain assumes control of the House Banking Committee. St. Germain is a strong opponent of deregulation.

The House Energy and Commerce Committee weighs in to keep banks out of insurance and securities underwriting.

Ideas
Policy Core
1. Efficiency, and the belief that market discipline is good for banking, although contested, is grafted onto the deep core beliefs.
2. Consumer service is grafted onto the long-held consumer-protection ethos.
3. Separation-by-function criteria are relaxed further.

Programmatic
4. The unit-banking ideal is weakened.
5. The dual-banking system is modified.
6. Cross-state mergers are allowed in select cases to head off financial-institution failure.
7. Cross-industry mergers are authorized to head off financial-institution failure.
8. Interest on checking is provided vis-à-vis money market demand accounts.
9. Thrift investment restrictions are relaxed.
10. All lending institutions are subject to universal capital requirements.

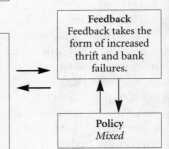

Feedback
Feedback takes the form of increased thrift and bank failures.

Policy
Mixed

Subsystem Politics
Competing coalitions consisting of consumer-borrowers and the securities and insurance industries, allied with small banks and thrifts, are arrayed against the ABA, bank regulators, and consumer-savers.

FIGURE 7.4   The dynamic of subsystem change: Garn–St. Germain, 1982

Increasingly shaky clientele support forced the FHLBB and St. Germain to explore policy alternatives along deregulatory lines. St. Germain sponsored legislation that involved some piecemeal tinkering with regulatory authority vis-à-vis failing institutions, and Garn pushed a more radical deregulatory solution (Gregg 1980c). In the end, events forced the House and Senate to compromise on the legislation known as Garn–St. Germain.

Garn–St. Germain broadened the powers of regulators to deal with failing institutions—allowing interstate and cross-industry mergers as a last resort. It also allowed interest on checking in the form of money market demand accounts offered by thrifts and banks, widened the investment opportunities for thrifts, and increased loan limits to single borrowers. Clearly the act challenged the core belief that banking was somehow different from other forms of commerce. Still, safety and soundness criteria remained a key part of the belief system—the largest part of the bill dealt with the means of handling and preventing financial-institution failure. The principle of protecting "other people's money," enshrined in deposit insurance, was reinforced through measures bolstering each of the deposit-insurance funds. In comparison to what was happening in other areas of economic regulation, the financial industry escaped the broad deregulation that overtook industries such as airlines, telecommunications, and trucking.

Still, the events surrounding the passage of Garn–St. Germain, and the act itself, highlight the break that was occurring with New Deal principles of regulation. Nonbank banks from the insurance and securities industries were able to block the extension of financial regulation to their banklike activities. In the past, there would have been little debate over the obvious solution of extending regulation to those engaged in such activity. Ironically, these same outsiders managed to prevent the encroachment on their home turf by banks through an appeal to New Deal prohibitions against such activity. The nonbank banks, then, were successful in both evading financial regulation and preventing unwanted competition.

Deregulation of the financial industry was clearly unfinished business in 1982—unfinished because events outside subsystem members' control were still unfolding; unfinished in that the truce between competing coalitions was but a short-term expedient; unfinished because the subsystem coalitions themselves were in a state of flux, as were the tenets of the belief system that had united subsystem players in their devotion to the New Deal regulatory regime; and finally, unfinished in that no interest was entirely satisfied with the patchwork system created by DIDMCA and Garn-St. Germain. The equilibrium established via legislation was to be short lived.

THE EMPEROR'S NEW CLOTHES, OR LEARNING TO LIVE WITH ADMINISTRATIVE DEREGULATION AND BANK FAILURE

The immediate result of the DIDMCA- and Garn–St. Germain–engineered stalemate was that the OCC and state regulators pursued deregulation on their own. The OCC used the "nonbank-bank loophole" to allow national banks to pursue a wide variety of investment opportunities theoretically prohibited banks by law. The loophole allowed banks to get rid of their commercial loan activity, maintain deposits and deposit insurance, and thus technically redefine themselves as non-banks. State regulators pursued an even more open form of deregulation. The "South Dakota loophole" allowed Citibank (and all comers) to purchase a state-chartered bank and use it to sell insurance out of state. Other states threatened to follow suit with credit card operations and similar endeavors.

The antideregulation coalition, consisting of small banks, savings and loans, and the FHLBB, was caught in a bind (see Figure 7.5). It was able to prevent further deregulation vis-à-vis legislation, but it was not strong enough to reimpose regulation or even slow the administrative deregulation pursued by national and state regulators. In an effort to curtail further deregulatory moves emanating from the Senate, the antideregulation coalition widened the scope of the conflict by enlisting the support of small securities firms and the insurance industry. These latter two were just as leery about competition from large banks in insurance and securities dealings as were thrifts and small banks. St. Germain invited John Dingell, the chair of the House Energy and Commerce Committee, to hold hearings on financial deregulation. By doing so, St. Germain was actually encouraging venue switching and the weakening of subsystem prerogatives in a desperate attempt to stop deregulation. This stalemate strategy could work only as long as the economic environment remained stable, a condition that was shaky at best. There was a dramatic rise in the number of bank and thrift failures in 1984 and 1985, followed by a record number of failures in 1987. When the cost of rescuing the FSLIC increased by a factor of six in 1988, it became clear the savings and loan situation required more than money or policy as usual.

Patching together an emergency bailout package proved no small feat. Whereas both chambers were in rough agreement on the general shape of the bailout and reform package, the size and composition of the conference committee indicated this was not subsystem policymaking as usual. The conference committee consisted of 102 legislators—8 from the Senate and 94 from the House. Three of the 8 Senate members and 20 of the 94 House participants came from their chamber's tax committees (Cranford 1989). This in and of itself was not so much a breach of banking turf, since a portion of the legislation was concerned with changing the tax laws affecting thrifts and banks. Rather, the fact that an additional 23 House members came from committees other than Banking or Ways and Means indicated that subsystem players were losing control over events.

Among the highlights of the bill reported out of conference were the creation of the Office of Thrift Supervision (OTS), under Treasury auspices, to replace the long-standing and suffering Federal Home Loan Bank Board and the formation of the Resolution Trust Corporation (RTC), under FDIC supervision, to manage the sale of real estate and other assets seized from failed thrifts. The change in institutional arrangements might seem the culmination of the long campaign for regulatory reform, but it was pretty much old wine in a new bottle. The hope-

Systemic Events
Economic Dislocation
Record failures of S&Ls bankrupt the FSLIC.

Interest rates skyrocket, further heightening disinter-mediation.

South Dakota loophole opens the door for national banks to pursue investment activities nominally prohib-ited by law.

FDIC is threatened with bankruptcy.

Party Politics
"Reagan revolution" divides Congress.

Institutional Conflict
House and Senate Banking Committees are at odds over deregulation.

John Dingell fights deregulation of banking from his base as chair of the House Energy and Commerce Com-mittee, seriously challenging the policy monopoly estab-lished by the Banking Committee.

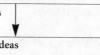

Feedback
Takes the form of increased competition and conflict among state and national regulators experimenting with new investment opportunities.

Ideas
Policy Core
1. Market discipline, with a modicum of regulation, is necessary to ensure efficiency in all financial services.
2. Consumer service is best met through widening the choices of investment opportunity.
3. Separation-by-function criteria are best met through tax breaks for mortgage lending.

Programmatic
4. Institute new capital requirements for all financial intermediaries.
5. Allow thrifts to organize securities affiliates to deal in securities market.
6. Ease branching prohibitions and separation-by-function regulation via new merger guidelines for failing institutions.
7. Remove regulation of interest rates.

Policy
Mixed

Subsystem Politics
Competing coalitions consisting of consumer-borrow-ers, and small securities and insurance firms, allied with small banks and thrifts, oppose regulator attempts to deregulate via administrative fiat.

FIGURE 7.5   The dynamic of subsystem change: Administrative deregulation, 1982–1990

lessly inept FHLBB was replaced by the OTS, but its head remained the same, as did its manner of operation.

On the regulatory reform side, the bill established new universal capital requirements for all lending institutions, raised the percent of funds invested in home mortgages necessary to qualify for a tax break, banned investments in junk bonds by thrifts but allowed such investment by separately capitalized affiliates, and added disclosure requirements under the Community Reinvestment Act. It also placed the financing of the FSLIC bailout in the budget. The first two provisions were clearly attempts to solidify New Deal regulatory elements, the fourth was a compromise between deregulators and New Dealers, and the third and fifth were the product of more contemporary political concerns sparked by the junk bond fiasco and charges of redlining lending practices.[1]

The legislation did little in the way of institutionalizing deregulation, yet it did not rule out further regulator-sponsored deregulation. Whereas the lack of legislature-induced policy change can be explained in part by the need to deal with the thrift insurance crisis, it can also be understood as a subsystem-generated stalemate. Quite simply, outsiders from the securities and insurance industries allied with the IBAA and thrift trade associations were adamantly opposed to deregulation and managed to stall for time.

To quote Yogi Berra, the 1990s were "déjà vu all over again." The deregulatory coalition was still hard at it, the New Deal adherents were fighting it tooth and nail, and all this occurred in the midst of yet another deposit-insurance crisis. This time it was a Congressional Budget Office study released in early 1991 and predicting the failure of 340 insured banks and the insolvency of the FDIC that formed the backdrop for the deregulatory debate (Cranford 1991d).

The coalition lineup assumed the three-ring format hinted at in the 1980s. A deregulatory coalition composed of the ABA, national bank regulators, large securities firms, and select members of the banking committees was joined by the president. Subsystem advocates of deregulation argued that legislating deregulation was the best means for returning the policymaking reins to the hands of subsystem players. The New Deal (antideregulation) coalition included the IBAA, USLSA, consumer advocates, and the chairs of the House and Senate Banking Committees. They castigated deregulation as "a package for Wall Street, crafted by former Wall Street operatives and consultants"—a none-too-subtle reference to Treasury secretary Brady's previous employment (Cranford 1991b). In their view, the beauty of New Deal regulation was that it allowed small and large banks to compete as equals, something deregulation would end.

The subsystem opponents of deregulation were loosely allied with a third coalition consisting of the insurance industry and smaller securities firms. Its legislative champion was the Democratic chair of the House Energy and Commerce Committee, John Dingell of Michigan. Dingell fought fiercely to protect the securities and insurance subsystem from a deregulation-sparked invasion by banks. The Dingell-led coalition occupied a curious position. Originally invited in by St.

Germain to head off the deregulatory coalition in the previous round of politicking, it now operated independently of St. Germain. Dingell fought to permanently alter the venue in which the Banking Committee was the primary institutional actor to one in which his Energy and Commerce Committee would control the debate.

Due to Dingell's efforts, the legislation was referred not only to the Banking Committee but to Energy and Commerce, Agriculture, Judiciary, and Ways and Means as well. Arguing that deregulatory proposals were a repeat of "the mistakes in policy that produced two of the greatest financial debacles in history: the market crash of 1929 and the savings and loan fiasco [of the 1980s]," Dingell produced a piece of legislation that was a return to New Deal principles of regulation (Cranford 1991g, 2608). The House voted to kill the measure, prompting the Senate to halt consideration of a similar measure so as to "study the aftermath" of the House incident. A narrowly focused bailout bill was eventually reported out of conference during the waning moments of the 102nd Congress, passed by both chambers, and signed into law a week short of Christmas.

DEREGULATION OF THE FINANCIAL INDUSTRY: ONLY THE STRONG SURVIVE

The story of financial deregulation illustrates the essential role of policy learning in programmatic change, learning that in turn was sparked by technological, economic, and political changes that upset carefully crafted subsystem arrangements. Some subsystem players' policy core beliefs were modified as a result of environmental changes and policy failures at the programmatic level. The New Deal view of markets as inherently destructive was replaced by an emphasis on markets as a superior mechanism of organizing business enterprises. Efficiency became an important value, not replacing equity entirely but at least as important as equity. Concentrations of economic power were to be managed rather than prohibited. Finally, consumer protection was redefined to include a service orientation in the form of a higher rate of return on investments, in addition to the New Deal goal of safeguarding deposits. These changes in turn gave rise to a variety of new programmatic objectives from ending interest-rate differentials enshrined in Regulation Q to easing branching and interstate banking prohibitions. All these were the logical programmatic manifestations of the new era of "full-service banking."

Still, the central tenet of New Deal banking, that the use of "other people's money" ought to be regulated, was maintained via safety and soundness principles. Indeed, the cartel-like arrangements institutionalized through Federal Reserve membership and deposit insurance remained unchanged. Although the separation-by-function principles enshrined in the New Deal were greatly modified, the retention of firewalls between investment and commercial banking, as well as tax breaks for home mortgages, preserved important elements of the New Deal system.

The key to policy change was the role played by regulators and the process of policy learning. Initially the Federal Reserve Board, Federal Deposit Insurance Corporation, the Office of the Comptroller of the Currency, and the Federal Home Loan Bank Board saw their primary duty as policing the boundaries established by the New Deal. Economic events altered this perspective. The interest-rate gap caused by inflation, technological change that made New Deal restrictions mere paper regulation, the entry of the nonbank banks as major competitors, and the increasing number of depository institution failures all forced a reassessment of New Deal provisions for ensuring safety and soundness. Regulators were among the first subsystem players to recognize the need for change, especially after their initial effort to extend regulation to the nonbank banks failed. Although the OCC under John Saxon was an extreme example of regulator-led deregulation, most regulators were advocates of incremental change in the programmatic features of the system.

Equally important, all resisted more radical calls for institutional change when it became clear such change could lead to the neglect of their particular clients' economic well-being. They were joined in their resistance by most legislators on the banking committees. Even as enthusiastic a deregulator as Jake Garn did not call for dismantling the institutional edifice of the financial subsystem.

In the end, a good deal of the pace and nature of regulatory reform was controlled by subsystem players. All attempts to create a single regulatory authority met with defeat, due principally to the opposition of regulators and regulated. The regulated recognized early on that any change in administrative organization could open the system to outsider influence, a fear that culminated in their opposition to Dingell's attempt to provide SEC oversight of banks' securities operations. In addition, the suspicion of most Banking Committee members of any presidential attempt to coordinate policy via the OCC, Treasury, and other regulators served to reinforce the inclination to resist administrative reform. The resistance of subsystem members to institutional change, whether or not they were part of the deregulatory or no-change coalitions, indicates a good deal of consensus with regard to these elements of the policy core.

In contrast, self-interest and a lack of consensus on programmatic matters produced a volatile mixture. Still, clashing self-interest alone was simply a necessary, not a sufficient, condition for policy change. Change occurred only after idea entrepreneurs—principally economists and regulators, were able to convince legislators and a portion of the regulated that change was inevitable. They did so by offering them "reasonable" explanations for the changing economic situation of financial intermediaries and then adding their solution to the existing regulatory mix. Thus deregulation was adopted in a form that suited the needs and beliefs of actors within the financial subsystem. Rather than the New Deal paradigm being replaced wholesale, elements were grafted onto the existing system, and the financial subsystem continued to thrive.

8

Conclusion: Subsystems as a Unit of Analysis

This concluding chapter offers a reprise of the subsystem framework developed in the opening chapter. Care is taken to both elucidate the major elements of the model and compare this explanation to other studies of the subsystem phenomenon.

WHO GETS WHAT

Subsystems and subsystem political variation are worthy topics of study because they provide an answer to Lasswell's query concerning "who gets what, when, and how." Subsystems produce policy that favors well-organized interests. This is not all that surprising a finding. Ted Lowi (1969) decried this phenomenon, and numerous observers have noted it since. This study modifies this simple truth with the observation that variation in interest group participation—subsystem politics—affects the calculus of winners and losers produced by the legislative process. Thus, like Bosso (1987), Baumgartner and Jones (1993), Eisner (1993), and Sabatier and Jenkins-Smith (1993), I argue that who is active in a subsystem has an important impact on what kind of goods that subsystem produces.

The tendency and ability of subsystems to produce distributive policy in which benefits are concentrated and costs diffuse is directly tied to the particular variant of subsystem politics in operation. As Chapter 5 demonstrates, bank-dominant politics produce a disproportionate share of legislation that benefits banks. Shake up the interest group mix with the addition of a president-led intrusion (transitory politics) or the actions of well-organized outsiders (competitive coalitions) and the policy outcomes take a redistributive or regulatory bent.

Still, despite the possibility and not infrequent occurrence of outsider participation, subsystems tend toward closure. That is, there appears to be a "natural" tendency for politics to return to something that resembles dominant coalitions. In the case of financial regulation, this means that some segment of the financial industry usually figures in as beneficiary. Thus the "who" portion of Lasswell's question invariably includes regulated interests, although it may include nonregulated interests as well.

Variation in subsystem politics has its largest impact on the "what" portion of the question. Although regulated interests or a faction of the regulated industry invariably receives something from most regulation, what it receives often depends on subsystem politics. Splits among the regulated, typical of transitory and competitive coalitions, are more likely to produce attempts at redistribution along with the extension of regulatory protections or goals sought by public interest groups or consumers of banking services. Thus the fulfillment of "outsider" goals is often dependent on a lack of harmony of interests among the regulated. The gravest threats to subsystem arrangements come from within—when private actors cannot reach agreement on essential policy questions. Such disagreement invites participation by nonmembers not bound by the beliefs that serve as the basis of subsystem arrangements. Outsider participation may tempt political sovereigns to permanently alter institutional arrangements and the nature of regulation.

It should come as no surprise that a key explanation of the staying power of subsystems has to do with the nature of interest group politics in the U.S. polity. Subsystems function as they do and continue to function because they serve the needs of powerful, organized interests. Financial-industry actors are the one constant through nearly 100 years of financial regulation. Quite simply, the regulated are in for the long haul, as the holding-company case (Chapter 6) demonstrates so nicely. Yet one cannot simply speak of financial regulation as captured. This is because the financial industry is not the only interest active within the political system.

As the partial deregulation of banking makes clear, alliances involving outsiders have dominated subsystem politics since the 1970s. Such alliances are not simply a recent phenomenon. Indeed, there are instances of similar politics throughout the history of financial regulation. The early attempts to form a Federal Reserve were joint efforts of industrial capital, farm interests, and banks. Similarly, much of New Deal regulation was backed by a coalition of business interests, consumers, and small banks suffering from the tight money policy promoted by large banks. Coinciding with the rise of public interest groups in the late 1960s, consumerism swept the financial subsystem in the 1970s. Subsystems, then, are not impervious to the demands of outside interests. Indeed, inviting in outsiders is a key means of gaining allies in inter-subsystem struggles (Sabatier and Jenkins-Smith 1993).

THE DYNAMIC OF SUBSYSTEM CHANGE: SYSTEMIC VARIABLES

Subsystems develop and evolve as a part of a larger political-economic system. Too often this obvious point is missed or forgotten in studies of subsystem politics. All subsystems attempt to effect closure on matters of concern to subsystem players; their ability to do so varies over time and across circumstances. Events in the larger environment play an important role in subsystem political change. In Chapter 1, building on the advocacy-coalition framework of Paul Sabatier and Hank Jenkins-Smith (1993), I developed a dynamic theory of subsystem politics suggesting that systemic events are filtered through the belief system(s) of interest group coalitions. The interpretation of these systemic events or stimuli may lead to learning and policy change on the part of subsystem insiders. Systemic events may attract outsiders to the subsystem, often after the costs of policy become clear, or elicit a response by other institutional players. We now turn to a consideration of the role of systemic variables—economic dislocation, institutional dynamics, party politics, and media attention—in shaping subsystem politics and policy outcomes.

Economic Dislocation

Economic downturns that directly impact the business of banking are perhaps the most stunning example of the effect of events in the larger environment on subsystem deal making. The rash of bank failures associated with various depressions and recessions at the turn of the century led to the formation of the Federal Reserve, the Great Depression gave rise to the New Deal regulatory structure, and the credit crunch of the 1970s sparked deregulatory discussion. In each of the preceding the performance of the economy was eventually linked to the performance of banking. In most instances there was a good deal of debate over the direction of causality, that is, whether banks were responsible for the sorry state of the economy or vice versa. But in no case was there any doubt that a link existed. This is because the business of banking is so intertwined with other kinds of business endeavors—from manufacturing to merchandising to real estate—that it always figures in any discussion of the economy and business, a discussion, it should be said, that involves a wider variety of interests than is normally involved in the formation of banking policy.

In addition to economic crises, changes in technology and markets also force reevaluation of key beliefs underlying the financial subsystem. The demise of localized economies and markets that accompanied the growth of industry in the nineteenth century forced the rethinking of unit-banking principles and led to the development of the Federal Reserve system. The savings and loan industry flourished with the growth of the home mortgage market following World War II and the inclusion of homeownership as a key piece of the American dream. Electronic banking, the outgrowth of technological changes affecting telecommunications and data processing, sparked the reevaluation of ideas concerning consumer protection and service in the latter half of the twentieth century. In each of the preceding the business of banking and, more to the point, beliefs about what banking entailed, underwent change. Change in beliefs caused by new economic opportunities, new customer demands, and new technology all lead to change in the cast of players involved in making bank policy.

Both the Federal Reserve and New Deal examples mentioned earlier illustrate an important phenomenon related to crises. When the action, or inaction, of subsystem players has an obvious detrimental effect on the system as a whole, one can expect participation by outsiders. Such participation often comes in the form of executive-led coalitions or outsiders invited in by a minority coalition. It may also involve a change in venue in which other committees hold hearings (as demonstrated in Chapter 4) or in which activity is switched to an entirely new institutional setting such as the courts or state legislatures, as was the case during the deregulatory drama of the 1980s (see also Baumgartner and Jones 1993). Thus the ability of a subsystem to maintain closure is often tied to the ability of regulated interests to perform policymaking functions satisfactorily.

Subsystems often do perform up to snuff. That is, they prove quite able to dispense goods and settle disputes out of the public eye during periods of economic growth or in less tumultuous times. The holding-company case in Chapter 6 is a nice example of economic variables, in this case the war and postwar economic boom, promoting the contraction of interest groups involved in engineering financial regulatory policy. The flip side of economic dislocation is made up of the long periods of economic tranquillity during which dominant coalitions reign supreme.

Institutional Dynamics

In addition to economically induced change, alteration in long-standing institutional arrangements are a potential spark of subsystem political change (see Eisner 1993; Baumgartner and Jones 1993; Sabatier and Jenkins-Smith 1993). The most likely candidate is a change in presidential administration, which often produces transitory coalitions. Presidents acting as agenda setters may intentionally or unintentionally threaten subsystem arrangements. Much of New Deal financial regulation appears to have been an afterthought. That is, it was part of the larger presidential project to right the economy (see Chapter 2). Deregulation began as a presidential project for administrative reform; this project snowballed into an effort at widespread policy change (Chapter 7). In both instances, presidents pursued policy goals that conflicted with some facet of existing subsystem arrangements. They were not so much interested in banking policy per se but rather in how it constrained economic policy and recovery in the former case or in how it was symptomatic of bothersome and inefficient economic regulation in the latter instance. Presidential intrusions are important stimulants, but they are also transitory phenomena; subsystem arrangements prove incredibly resistant to presidential overtures for change. A good deal of this resilience can be explained by the institutional arrangements that serve as the basis of any subsystem.

Two sets of institutional arrangements in particular are important—the congressional committee system and the network of administrative agencies that are the institutional embodiment of regulatory beliefs and goals. The case-study chapters highlight the importance of congressional committees in the formation and maintenance of the financial subsystem. From House Banking Committee chair Charles Fowler's early attempts at currency stabilization at the turn of the century to Jake Garn and Fernand St. Germain's efforts in the 1980s, the banking committees have been an institutional bulwark of the financial subsystem. All attempts at institutional change must eventually pass through the oversight committees. Indeed, the banking committees pursue coalition formation and maintenance as a major objective. Thus although banking legislators are members of distinct coalitions, they are also bridge builders between coalitions and the political system at large.

It is when legislators become caught up in conflict among industry factions that the institutional safeguard provided by the banking committees breaks down. The split between the House and Senate committees provided an opportunity for the president to step in during the formation of the Federal Reserve and the New Deal systems. Infighting between the House Banking Committee and its Financial Institutions Subcommittee presented a similar opportunity during the deregulation debate of the 1980s and 1990s. In such cases regulators are often the last institutional safeguard of subsystem arrangements.

Regulators are called on to play two roles in the subsystem drama—policy expert and industry manager. The two are of course interrelated. As industry managers, their primary role is looking after the financial interests and health of their private-sector charges. Thus the OCC is on constant guard lest state-chartered banks be allowed business opportunities denied nationally chartered institutions. Similarly, the FHLBB continuously guarded the savings and loan industry against encroachment by commercial banks. In addition to protecting their industry's turf, regulators as managers are also expected to insulate the regulated from their own self-destructive behavior. Competition is managed, investment is controlled, and prudence is required. Indeed, the FDIC is ever vigilant in protecting depositors' funds; the Fed looks after capitalization and reserve requirements.

As policy experts, regulators are expected to be able to anticipate and interpret external shocks that threaten subsystem arrangements. As such they are key players in the subsystem drama, not the mere pawns of private interests or servants of legislators. Even when they pursue management functions, the more likely scenario for the OCC and FHLBB after the New Deal, they are still concerned with system-maintenance questions that distinguish them from the regulated. The mismanagement—quite simply, lax regulation—of thrifts by the FSLIC in the 1980s was clear warning of the hazards of complacency and too servile attempts to meet the short-term goals of self-interested industry actors.[1]

Party Politics

No subsystem wants to be caught up in the dog-eat-dog world of party politics. When a subsystem's policy preserve becomes the subject of party-based discussion, subsystem autonomy goes out the window. For the most part the financial subsystem is fairly well insulated from the immediate effects of party politics. The distributive nature of much of financial regulation goes a long way in lessening the impact of partisan politics on events in the financial subsystem. This does not mean the subsystem is immune to partisan changes in the White House or Congress. Rather, such change is usually systemwide if it has a dramatic impact on the shape of financial regulation (Sabatier and Jenkins-Smith 1993).

As Table 8.1 demonstrates, the most dramatic changes in financial regulation occur during periods in which both chambers of Congress and the executive are subject to a change in party control. The creation of the national bank system, the birth of the Federal Reserve, and the New Deal banking reforms all coincide with shifts in party control of the executive and both houses of Congress. In other cases—the holding-company example and the partial deregulation of banking, where party change affects only a part of the political system—the policy results are less dramatic. So, for example, party change that produces a new chair of one of the banking committees may have an effect on the type of policy pursued, as the cases of Charles Tobey and holding-company regulation in the 1940s and Jake Garn and deregulation in the 1980s so nicely demonstrate. But party change in one branch of the government does not have the radical impact of systemwide shifts in party control.

TABLE 8.1   Party Politics and Policy Initiatives

Act	Executive	House	Senate
Currency Act of 1863 and National Bank Act of 1864	change (Dem to GOP)	change (Dem to GOP)	change (Dem to GOP)
Federal Reserve Act, 1913	change (GOP to Dem)	change (GOP to Dem)	change (GOP to Dem)
New Deal reforms 1933, 1935	change (GOP to Dem)	change (GOP to Dem)	change (GOP to Dem)
Bank Holding Company Act, 1956	change (Dem to GOP)	no change[a]	no change[a]
Hunt Commission and *FINE* Study, 1973–1975	no change	no change	no change
DIDMCA, Garn–St. Germain, 1980–1982	change (Dem to GOP)	no change	change (Dem to GOP)

[a] During the period indicated there was actually a good deal of change, but since the period began and ended under a Democrat-controlled Congress, it is classified as a no-change period.

Media Attention

Like Baumgartner and Jones (1993), this study finds that increased issue salience is associated with changes in participation patterns in the financial subsystem. Increased media scrutiny of banking policy is accompanied by competition among interest groups, legislators, and the president for a place at the banking table. As coverage becomes more critical of the conduct of banking policy, politics become more competitive. Thus the adage about no news being good news is especially apt for subsystem players trying to insulate policymaking from outsider scrutiny or participation.

SUBSYSTEM POLITICAL VARIATION: INTERNAL VARIABLES

The preceding variables are exogenous in the sense that they account for changes in the environment in which subsystems are nested. Change in environmental variables alone, although often a necessary condition for subsystem political change, does not necessarily produce policy change (see Brown and Stewart 1993). Rather, it is the interaction of these system-level variables with endogenous variables that may lead to policy change. Quite simply, if the preceding systemic variables are to have an impact on the course of financial regulation, they must affect the composition and the beliefs of the various coalitions active in any particular subsystem.

Interest Groups

As noted earlier, organized interests are at the heart of subsystems, the policy process, and the American polity. Although subsystems are insulated from the larger environment, this study demonstrates that they are not immune to systemwide changes in the polity. Such change is most visible in the identity of interest groups active in various facets of the legislative process and manifests itself in different forms of coalitional politics—dominant, transitory, and competitive.

An important change contributing to a shift in subsystem politics involves changes in the composition of the interest group universe. Although the example often given of this type of change is the public interest group revolution in the 1960s (see Gais, Peterson, and Walker 1984), such change occurs periodically (see Eisner 1993). The regular cycles of increased political activity by interest groups and political movements pursuing their vision of the public interest make it difficult for subsystems to pursue policy as usual (see Eisner 1993; Harris and Milkis 1989). In the realm of banking, the creation of the Federal Reserve, the New Deal changes with regard to deposit insurance, truth-in-lending legislation of the 1970s, and full-service banking of the 1980s are all the result of popular demands for policy change. Each were pursued by coalitions of interests previously uninvolved in banking policy. Still, the impact of change in the composition of the interest group universe is filtered through institutional arrangements that lie at the heart of the financial subsystem. Rather than causing the abandonment of established relationships, public interest group demands are grafted onto existing beliefs—which brings us to the role of ideas.

Beliefs

The self-interest of private actors alone cannot explain the remarkable staying power of subsystem arrangements. If self-interest were the only basis of the belief system that underlies subsystems, one could argue that subsystem disintegration is inevitable (as do Hammond and Knott 1988). Rather, material self-interest is but one facet of the variety of beliefs that lie at the heart of the financial subsystem.

The case studies of the formation of the Federal Reserve system, bank holding-company regulation, and partial deregulation illustrate the important role played by ideas in the maintenance and alteration of subsystem arrangements. Technological change and economic events provide a new set of incentives and challenges for subsystem players. They may produce demands for alterations in standing policy, as well as anomalies that current beliefs cannot explain. As such they are cause for reassessment of programmatic options and often policy beliefs. Similarly, changes in party control of the executive or legislature and in interinstitutional relations prompt reassessment of beliefs. Still, none of the preceding "force" change. Rather, they offer an opportunity for subsystem players to offer new interpretations of, or explanations for, events that affect subsystem-authored arrangements.

Thus, as suggested by Sabatier and Jenkins-Smith (1993), policy change occurs as a result of policy learning. Although policy core beliefs are slow to change, alteration is a real possibility. The relaxation of some separation-by-function criteria during deregulation, the similar reaction to the holding-company phenomenon in the 1950s, and the current debate over banks underwriting insurance are all examples of the mutability of core beliefs. Yet each also demonstrates the staying power of core beliefs. Regulation still distinguishes between intermediaries in the business of mortgage lending and those who engage primarily in commercial lending, banks cannot enter a variety of endeavors open to other forms of business, and no one is suggesting banks are the same as insurers. Rather than completely abandoning core beliefs, all the preceding required some change in core beliefs accompanied by a change in their programmatic manifestations.

Indeed, change in beliefs is a necessary requisite for policy change and may even result in a change in subsystem politics. It is the combination of material interests served by and policy core beliefs enshrined in institutional structures that give subsystem arrangements their staying power. Programmatic elements of the financial subsystem belief system are subject to constant reevaluation and tinkering. Core beliefs, in contrast, are more stable, subject to examination under "unusual" circumstances—severe economic downturns, systemwide political change, and the like—and less likely candidates for radical change.

Political change, then, is a product of systemic effects filtered through existing institutional arrangements, is shaped by dominant beliefs, and is buffeted by interest group demands. None of the preceding alone or in concert automatically produce change. Rather, they interact with, shape, and are shaped by the existing subsystem mix of beliefs, interest groups, and systemic variables.

SUBSYSTEMS AS WAVERING EQUILIBRIUMS

At the heart of this book is the notion that subsystem politics vary over time and that such variation produces different sorts of policy outcomes. The argument that subsystem politics vary over time is not all that revolutionary. Several recent observers of the subsystem phenomenon have toyed with the notion (most notably Bosso 1987; McCool 1989, 1990; Thurber 1991; Sabatier and Jenkins-Smith 1993), and this study builds on this foundation. In one of the most impressive efforts to date, Frank Baumgartner and Bryan Jones (1993) argue that the American political system, and the subsystems that are an integral part of that system, resemble a punctuated equilibrium. According to Baumgartner and Jones, any subsystem-induced equilibrium is subject to rapid and radical change during particular periods characterized by a burst of interest in the policy area on the part of public and private actors.

The story of banking policy offers qualified support for the notion of a punctuated equilibrium. There are several periods of heightened salience that are accompanied by an increase in the variety of interest groups and institutional players involved in banking policy. Yet none of these result in a radical change in subsystem arrangements. Rather, subsystem politics waver—allowing outsiders their day in the sun and thus avoiding dramatic restructuring (the punctuating act identified by Baumgartner and Jones [1993]). New ideas or programs are grafted onto existing beliefs, outsiders gain their piece of the programmatic pie, and the financial subsystem moves on to the next series of challenges.

Subsystem politics, then, often shift from one point on the subsystem continuum to another as a result of the interaction of environmental stimuli and internal activities. In the realm of financial regulation there appears to be a cycle of sorts, with politics wavering between bank-dominant, transitory, and competitive. It also appears that over time a wider variety of interests have become involved in subsystem policymaking. This cycling between closed and open politics mirrors changes in the polity at large. The broadening of the interest group universe has been described as the public interest revolution (Gais, Peterson, and Walker 1984; Scholzman and Tierney 1986; Petracca 1992), the birth of social regulation (Pertschuk 1982; Gormley 1983; Noll and Owen 1983; Derthick and Quirk 1985; Meier 1985; Reagan 1987), or regime change (Eisner 1993; Harris and Milkis 1989). It should come as little surprise that systemic changes have financial-subsystem repercussions. Several observers of subsystems operating in realms as diverse as agriculture and nuclear power have noted similar phenomena (Bosso 1987; Balogh 1991; Baumgartner and Jones 1993). Indeed, one might suggest that subsystems unable to adapt are subject to disintegration (Thurber 1991; Baumgartner and Jones 1993).

Another important feature of the wavering equilibrium is its interinstitutional nature. Subsystems are a bicameral affair in which both House and Senate committees serve as important institutional foundations. Chapters 2, 6, and 7, as well as the mapping exercise in Chapter 3, demonstrate that politics also waver as one moves from the Senate to the House. This bicameral feature provides a safety valve in which interests frozen out of one forum can have a go at policymaking in the other. Thus, the temptation for any particular interest to abandon the subsystem forum is greatly decreased. The bicameral nature of subsystems is too often neglected by those studying policy monopolies and should be considered in all future studies. Not only does it explain subsystems' longevity, it is an important variant of venue switching.

The Method to the Madness

A central concern of this study is developing a means of getting at subsystem political variation that is more systematic than previous efforts that rely on historically rich case studies alone (some of the most recent and excellent examples include Bosso 1987; Browne 1988; Balogh 1991). This is not to suggest that historical studies are an inferior approach or a thing of the past. Rather, like any particular approach, they have limits when employed as the sole method of research (see Goggin 1986). Indeed, historical treatment of banking policy is essential for an understanding of the ideas that lie at the heart of subsystem arrangements. The historical vantage also allows one to compare various attempts at restructuring subsystem arrangements, noting what is changing and, more important, what remains the same. Without the attention to detail and context provided by historical analysis, one might mistake an incremental shift in subsystem arrangements for radical change. Thus in this study I have combined historical analysis with the construction of participation profiles to offer a portrait of subsystem politics that has both breadth and depth.

Let me make a final case for the utility of subsystems as a unit of analysis and for the particular approach of this book. It is popular to dismiss the end product of the policy process as meaningless, biased, or so much smoke and mirrors. Indeed, the more pessimistic variants of the subsystem framework—iron triangle and capture—have been put to such use all too frequently (Edelman 1979; Ferejohn 1983; Fiorina 1977; and Posner 1974). Still, subsystems are where the action is; this study demonstrates that all too well. They are also not impermeable. Congressional committees, which serve as the institutional bedrock of subsystem relations, can and do change their legislative routine in response to external stimuli (see Chapter 4). They also vary policy outputs as a result of increased interest group activity (Chapter 5). Whereas subsystems are functional islands in the policy sea, their topography is subject to system-induced change. They can and do function as exercises in special interest government—the bank-dominant coalition scenario. Yet outsiders ranging from the members of transitory coalitions (the president, academics, stray legislators) to long-term competitors (consumers, business interests, and the like) make a difference. This study demonstrates that and offers an explanation of how and when this is likely to occur.

Updating the traditional interest group focus of subsystem studies with attention to belief systems offers an explanation for the staying power of subsystem arrangements, as well as their susceptibility to change. The addition of participation profiles as an indicator of political variation allows one to lengthen the time frame under study. It also offers a more systematic, easily replicated indicator of interest group activity that documents subsystem variation. The argument that subsystems are a useful unit of analysis in understanding the course of public policy should not be read as a simple rehash of the interest-group-liberalism argument. Rather, it is meant to turn observers' attention to the locus of a good deal of action in the polity. It is also offered as an amendment to those who hailed the death of subsystems.

Finally, in the case of regulation in the financial subsystem, whereas interest politics have undergone dramatic changes since the mid-1970s, institutional arrangements and beliefs that lie at the heart of subsystem relationships have been slower to change. Whether this is true of other subsystems, something I strongly suspect, is a question for future investigation.

Notes

CHAPTER ONE

1. I know of no work, however, arguing that Harold Lasswell was a pluralist.

2. Among those who use the iron triangle variant of subsystem politics in the study of policymaking are Griffith 1939; Bernstein 1955; Maass 1951; Scher 1960; Long 1962; Cater 1964; Freeman 1955, 1965; Lowi 1969; Redford 1969; Davidson 1977; and Fiorina 1977. Advocates of capture, or the economic school, include Stigler 1971; Posner 1974; Peltzman 1976; Owen and Braeutigam 1978; Noll and Owen 1983.

3. See Cater 1964; Freeman 1965; Fenno 1973; Ferejohn 1974 and 1983; Fiorina 1977; Davidson 1977; Shepsle 1978; Dodd and Schott 1979; Smith and Deering 1984; and Hall and Grofman 1990.

4. The notion of competitive coalitions combines the insights of Sabatier and Jenkins-Smith's (1993) advocacy-coalition framework with work by Baumgartner and Jones (1993), Balogh (1991), and Bosso (1987). The latter three examine the activities of outside interests in a variety of policy areas. Baumgartner and Jones focus on attempts by competitors to switch the venue in which agendas are addressed in areas as diverse as the regulation of drugs, smoking, and nuclear energy. Balogh documents the breakup of the nuclear subsystem, an event due in part to increasing challenges from outsiders.

5. This distinction, although inspired by Sabatier and Jenkins-Smith (1993), is not the same as their distinction between policy core and secondary aspects.

CHAPTER TWO

1. Much of the material on the development of the Federal Reserve system is taken from the excellent histories by Wiebe 1963, West 1977, White 1983, and Livingston 1986.

2. An important feature of the first national banking system was the arrangement by which smaller, primarily rural banks were required to maintain a fraction of their deposits in a reserve fund at select national banks. These reserve city banks, forced to pay interest on reserves, speculated with the funds so as to maximize their profit margins. Problems arose when downturns in the securities market coincided with increased demands for currency. Smaller institutions that attempted to draw on their reserve funds to meet the demands of depositors placed reserve city banks in a bind. Reserve city banks were caught short, as were unit banks, when depositors engaged in a run on all banks. The result was depositor panic and bank failure that reverberated throughout the system.

3. A brief survey of the *Annals of the American Academy of Social and Political Science* illustrates this trend. Whereas the issue of the journal prior to the panic (volume 1, 1890–1891) contains no discussion of currency reform, the latter numbers of the second

volume (1892–1893) contain articles by A. B. Hepburn, J. H. Walker, and Horace White and by additional authors who discuss the issue of currency reform and inelasticity.

4. For a more detailed discussion see West 1974; White 1983.

5. The notion of an emerging corporate class is developed and discussed in Livingston 1986. He presents a fascinating account of the emergence of the coalition whose ideas were eventually enshrined in the Federal Reserve Act, but he begins his account in the middle of the story (the Indianapolis convention). He ignores the impact of the Baltimore convention, which served as the basis for the Indianapolis convention. The notion of a corporate class demanding bank reform is a bit overly deterministic and misses the significant role played by select regulators and bankers in defining the problem in the 1870s, as well as the ability of bankers to shape the regulation to serve their ends.

6. Contemporary advocates of reform criticized the NMC, arguing that Aldrich had created it so he could control, and presumably sidetrack, any serious attempts at reform (West 1974, 68). Yet according to West, Aldrich became a convert of German banking practice and deserted his defense of bond-secured notes after a trip to Europe intended to investigate European central banking. Despite this conversion, the commission was slow to act on the matter of reform and was dissolved in 1911 (West 1974, 69). Although the Aldrich bill was eventually introduced in Congress and was no doubt a product of commission deliberations, the two-year space between its introduction and Aldrich's change of heart led many to suspect the senator was simply buying time for banking interests.

7. Clearinghouses were large money-center banks that processed, or cleared, the drafts of smaller institutions.

8. I borrow from the accounts of Kennedy 1973 and Burns 1974 in telling the story of New Deal reforms.

9. Discounting refers to the interest rate at which banks can borrow money from a Reserve bank, in this case the NCC. The Reserve bank deducts the interest from the amount borrowed at the time the loan is made, "discounting" the interest from the total amount of the loan.

10. Branches are bank offices owned by a single financial intermediary that allow that intermediary to conduct business in more than one geographic location. The controversy over branching arose as a result of those who favored a narrow reading of the National Bank Act and a literal understanding of what was involved in chartering a financial intermediary. Branching opponents argued unit banking was just that: One charter produced one bank office—no more and no less. The arguments against multiple offices, or branches, are nearly as old as banking itself, and uniquely American.

11. Despite the passage of the 1933 bank bill, the ABA continued to pressure the administration to postpone or abandon the insurance scheme throughout 1933. Fred I. Kent, of the New York Fed, acted as the ABA liaison to the White House, advising FDR that it was the "belief [of the ABA] that this law, if carried out might menace the whole recovery Act" (Burns 1974, 125). The ABA found Roosevelt unwilling, indeed unable, to abandon the insurance scheme, so it switched its energies to Congress. The Legislative Committee of the ABA advised its membership that the banking bill had lacked the wholehearted support of the president and the Congress as a whole. Rather, it was viewed as the special creature of several members of Congress and thus perceived as vulnerable to some intense lobbying by bankers (ABA, *Reports of the 59th Annual Convention*, 1933, 8; Burns 1974, 126). A number of editorials in *Bankers Magazine* called for an organized effort on the part of bankers to influence the implementation of the Banking Act as well as to influence the de-

sign of future legislation. The ABA effort paid off with the extension of the Temporary Deposit Insurance Fund in 1934 rather than the establishment of a permanent fund (Burns 1974, 127). The requirement that participant banks eventually join the Fed was dropped from a House version of a bill that increased the amount of insurance coverage. This was eventually amended to give participants until 1937 to decide whether to join the Federal Reserve or drop insurance (Burns 1974, 128).

12. Open-market operations allow the Fed to raise or lower the supply of money using something other than interest rates. Selling securities decreases the amount of money in circulation (the Fed "takes" money out of circulation from those who purchase securities); the Fed purchase of securities increases the supply of money (Kettl 1986, 5).

CHAPTER THREE

1. Hamm (1986) was interested in looking for variation in subsystem politics across policy areas at a single point in time. He examined six committees in the Colorado legislature with the intent of determining if different policy areas exhibit a different type of politics. In a similar exercise, I looked for variation across policy subtype—commercial banking, savings and loans, Federal Reserve monetary policy, consumer protection, and systemwide issues. The goal was to track any variation due to particular types of financial policy or actors being regulated in a fashion similar to Hamm's examination of different policy types. Although some variation was found, the results were mixed at best and are not reported here. Building on Hamm, I add a longitudinal element, examining hearings between 1919 and 1988.

CHAPTER FOUR

1. Agenda building is too often assumed to be the domain of the president alone. Presidents are instrumental as agenda builders, but they are rarely very involved in the financial subsystem (see Schroedel 1994). Indeed, as the New Deal case so nicely illustrated in Chapter 2, subsystems try to insulate themselves from the president as agenda setter with varying degrees of success.

2. Information on bills introduced was gathered from the *Congressional Record* for the years 1919 (the 66th Congress) through 1988 (the 100th Congress). The *Congressional Record* was also used to track the legislative history of bills—whether they were reported from committee, their fate on the floor and in the other chamber, and whether they became law. All told, some 4,159 bills were introduced in the period in question: 2,949 in the House, 1,210 in the Senate.

Only those bills that dealt with matters affecting domestic financial intermediaries—banks, thrifts, credit unions, mutual savings banks—and the conduct of U.S. monetary policy by the Federal Reserve were included in the counts for the House and Senate. Bills dealing exclusively with other types of financial intermediaries such as securities firms and investment banks were not included in the data set. The count includes all such bills, irrespective of the particular committee to which they were referred.

3. The figures for the tone of coverage, positive or negative, closely tracked the total story figure in most instances and are not reported.

4. I am indebted to Paul Sabatier for pointing out this key difference.

5. This turns out to be true in the case of financial regulation, where the House passes 74.2 percent of all legislation reported from committee and the Senate approves of 75.5 percent. Variation among the different subsystem political scenarios was almost nonexistent with dominant coalitions of either variety indistinguishable from one another and the chamber average.

CHAPTER FIVE

1. Only the statistical results for competitive and bank-dominant politics are reported given the small number of cases of transitory coalitions and the resulting unreliability of the significance tests.

2. As was the case at the reporting stage, although the results for all three variants in the Senate are reported, statistical tests of significance are for the bank-dominant and competitive types only. The small n for transitory coalitions made the results of such tests unreliable.

CHAPTER SIX

1. Under the 1933 legislation, holding companies that included member banks were required to register with the Federal Reserve Board. Board permission was required before registered companies could vote their stock interest in affiliated banks. Voting permits were granted only if all banks associated with the holding company agreed to examination by the Fed, divested themselves of securities affiliates, and met the reserve requirements of the Fed.

2. That Eccles disapproved of the "kill" facet of the original holding-company legislation was a surprise to few. Before joining the Federal Reserve, Eccles headed one of the more successful bank holding companies in the West. Still, the move by the Fed chair to bring holding-company operations under federal regulation was an important first step in gaining legitimacy for the proposition within the financial subsystem. This was not only a banker calling for increased regulation, it was a holding-company banker arguing the time had come for some type of regulation.

3. The Senate hearings make clear the principal role played by the Fed in the engineering of the Tobey bill. Indeed, at the opening of the hearing Tobey praised Eccles for his role in constructing the bill.

4. The degree to which S. 2577 was a done deal is obvious when one examines the hearings. Most of the time in what is an unusually brief hearing is taken up by Transamerica making one last, futile stand against regulation. Robertson abandoned the usual decorum shown witnesses, castigating Transamerica for its use of bullying tactics in its pressure campaign aimed at sinking the bill. In addition the subcommittee chair accused Transamerica of deception after it introduced a "neutral" study conducted by a nonprofit think tank—the Stanford Research Institute. The institute was not associated with Stanford University, although Transamerica tried to pass it off as such. Rather, it was the creation of Transamerica, its sole client (Senate 1956, 68–70). Following the airing of the Transamerica objections, the remainder of the hearing was taken up by short endorsements of the bill by the various subsystem participants.

CHAPTER SEVEN

1. Junk bonds were just what their name implied. They offered the possibility of high rates of return on investments of questionable worth and stability. Perfected by Michael Milkin, they led to the bankruptcies of several investment firms and investors, leading to a prison sentence for Milkin. The Community Reinvestment Act was an attempt to force the increasingly regional and national lenders not to forget local communities in their lending activities.

CHAPTER EIGHT

1. Picking on the FSLIC is like beating a dead horse. Still, one can argue that more vigilant policing of investments in commercial real estate, energy futures, speculative ventures, and higher capitalization requirements would have gone a long way toward minimizing the severity of the savings and loan crises in the 1980s.

References

Aberbach, Joel D., and Bert A. Rockman. 1978. "Bureaucrats and Clientele Groups: A View from Capitol Hill." *American Journal of Political Science* 22: 818–832.

Anderson, Clay J. 1965. *A Half Century of Federal Reserve Policymaking, 1914–1964.* Philadelphia: Federal Reserve Bank of Philadelphia.

Anderson, James E. 1962. *The Emergence of the Modern Regulatory State.* Washington, D.C.: Public Affairs Press.

Anderson, James E., David W. Brady, Charles S. Bullock, and Joseph Stewart. 1984. *Public Policy and Politics in America.* Monterey, Calif.: Brooks/Cole.

Arnold, R. Douglas. 1979. *Congress and the Bureaucracy: A Theory of Influence.* New Haven: Yale University Press.

Baker, Ross K. 1989. *House and Senate.* New York: W. W. Norton.

Balogh, Brian. 1991. *Chain Reaction.* Cambridge: Cambridge University Press.

Baumgartner, Frank R., and Bryan D. Jones. 1991. "Agenda Dynamics and Policy Subsystems." *Journal of Politics* 53(1):1044–1074.

_____. 1993. *Agendas and Instability in American Politics.* Chicago: University of Chicago Press.

Bequai, August. 1981. *The Cashless Society: EFTs at the Crossroads.* New York: John Wiley.

Bernstein, Marver H. 1955. *Regulating Business by Independent Commission.* Princeton: Princeton University Press.

Berry, William D. 1982. "Theories of Regulatory Impact." *Policy Studies Review* (February):436–441.

_____. 1984. "An Alternative to the Capture Theory of Regulation." *American Journal of Political Science* 28:524–558.

Bibby, John F., and Roger Davidson. 1967. "The Congressional Committee." In John F. Bibby and Roger Davidson, eds., *On Capitol Hill: Studies in the Legislative Process.* New York: Holt, Rinehart and Winston, pp. 170–196.

Blakely, Steve. 1986a. "Heavily Lobbied Banking Bills Remain Stalled in Rules Panel." *Congressional Quarterly Weekly Report* (March 1):530.

_____. 1986b. "'States Rights' Threatens Bank-Bailout Plan." *Congressional Quarterly Weekly Report* (May 17):1108.

_____. 1986c. "Panel Votes Bare Bones Bill to Aid FSLIC, Troubled Banks." *Congressional Quarterly Weekly Report* (August 16):1893.

_____. 1986d. "Non-Bank Bank Controversy Blocks Key Legislation." *Congressional Quarterly Weekly Report* (September 13):2143–2146.

_____. 1987. "Panel Approves $5 Billion FSLIC Reserve Plan." *Congressional Quarterly Weekly Report* (April 4):635–636.

Bond, Jon R. 1979. "Oiling the Tax Committee in Congress, 1900–1974: Subgovernment Theory, the Overrepresentation Hypothesis, and the Oil Depletion Allowance." *American Journal of Political Science* 23(November):651–664.

Bosso, Christopher J. 1987. *Pesticides and Politics: The Life Cycle of a Public Issue.* Pittsburgh: University of Pittsburgh Press.

Bowden, Elbert V. 1980. *Revolution in Banking.* Richmond, Va.: Robert F. Dame.

Brown, Anthony E., and Joseph Stewart Jr. 1993. "Competing Advocacy Coalitions, Policy Evolution, and Airline Deregulation." In Paul Sabatier and Hank Jenkins-Smith, eds., *Policy Change and Learning: An Advocacy Coalition Approach.* Boulder: Westview Press.

Browne, William P. 1988. *Private Interests, Public Policy, and American Agriculture.* Lawrence: University Press of Kansas.

Burns, Helen. 1974. *The American Banking Community and the New Deal Banking Reforms.* Westport: Greenwood Press.

Campbell, John L. 1988. *Collapse of an Industry: Nuclear Power and the Contradictions of U.S. Policy.* Ithaca, N.Y.: Cornell University Press.

Cargill, Thomas F., and Gillian G. Garcia. 1985. *Financial Reform in the 1980s.* Stanford: Stanford University Press.

Cary, William L. 1967. *Politics and the Regulatory Agencies.* New York: McGraw-Hill.

Cater, Douglas. 1964. *Power in Washington.* New York: Random House.

Cobb, Roger W. 1973. "The Belief-Systems Perspective: An Assessment of a Framework." *Journal of Politics* 35(February):121–153.

Cobb, Roger W., and Charles D. Elder. 1983. *Participation in American Politics: The Dynamics of Agenda Building.* Baltimore: Johns Hopkins University Press.

Cobb, Roger W., Jennie Keith-Ross, and Marc Ross. 1976. "Agenda Building as a Comparative Political Process." *American Political Science Review* 70(March):126–138.

Colton, Kent W., and Kenneth W. Kraemer. 1980. *Computers and Banking.* New York: Plenum Press.

Compton, Eric N. 1983. *Inside Commercial Banking.* New York: John Wiley.

Conte, Christopher. 1979. "A Reluctant Congress Faces a New Debate on Banking Laws." *Congressional Quarterly Weekly Report* (July 7):1364–1369.

Corey, 1930. *The House of Morgan.* New York: G. Howard Watt.

Cranford, John R. 1989. "102 Conferees Appointed on S&L Bill." *Congressional Quarterly Weekly Report* (June 24):1530.

_____. 1991a. "Financial System's Wounds May Only Be Bandaged." *Congressional Quarterly Weekly Report* (February 2):284–289.

_____. 1991b. "Administration Spells Out Plan to Reform Financial System." *Congressional Quarterly Weekly Report* (February 9):357–361.

_____. 1991c. "Bush Proposal Starts Debate on Future of State Banks." *Congressional Quarterly Weekly Report* (April 6):843–849.

_____. 1991d. "Hill Maneuvers Threaten Delay of Massive Overhaul Bill." *Congressional Quarterly Weekly Report* (July 13):1882.

_____. 1991e. "Big Banks Win First Round in Pursuit of New Powers." *Congressional Quarterly Weekly Report* (June 29):1732–1736.

_____. 1991f. "Riegle's Bill Bruised but Intact As Tense Markup Concludes." *Congressional Quarterly Weekly Report* (August 3):2134–2135.

Cranford, John R., and Alissa J. Rubin. 1991. "Panel Members Put Obstacles in Way of Overhaul Bill." *Congressional Quarterly Weekly Report* (September 14):2608.

Dahl, Robert. 1961. *Who Governs?* New Haven: Yale University Press.

Davidson, Roger H. 1977. "Breaking Up Those 'Cozy Triangles': An Impossible Dream?" In Susan Welch and John G. Peters, eds., *Legislative Reform and Public Policy.* New York : Praeger.

_____. 1989. *Congress and Its Members.* 3rd ed. Washington, D.C.: Congressional Quarterly Press.

Davis, Andrew M. 1910 (1980). *The Origin of the National Bank System.* New York: Arno Press.

DeGregorio, Christine. 1990. "Congressional Hearings Revisited." Paper presented at the Annual Meeting of the Midwest Political Science Association, the Palmer House, Chicago, Illinois, April 4–8.

Department of the Treasury. 1873. *United States Government Annual Report.* Washington, D.C.

Derthick, Martha, and Paul J. Quirk. 1985. *The Politics of Deregulation.* Washington, D.C.: Brookings Institution.

Dodd, Lawrence C., and Richard L. Schott. 1979. *Congress and the Administrative State.* New York: John Wiley.

Dubnick, Mel, and Alan R. Gitelson. 1982. "Regulatory Policy Analysis." *Policy Studies Review* (February):423–435.

Eads, George C., and Michael Fix. 1984. *The Reagan Regulatory Strategy.* Washington, D.C.: Urban Institute.

Eccles, Marriner with S. Hyman, ed. 1951. *Beckoning Frontiers.* New York: Alfred Knopf.

Edelman, Murray. 1979. *American Politics.* Lexington, Mass.: Heath.

Eisner, Marc Allen. 1990. *Antitrust and the Triumph of Economics.* Chapel Hill: University of North Carolina Press.

_____. 1993. *Regulatory Politics in Transition.* Baltimore: Johns Hopkins University Press.

Fainsod, Merle. 1940. "Some Reflections on the Nature of the Regulatory Process." *Public Policy* (1):297–323.

Federal Deposit Insurance Corporation. 1996. *Annual Report.* Washington, D.C.: Office of Public Information, FDIC.

Fenno, Richard F. 1962. "The House Appropriations Committee as a Political System." *American Political Science Review* 56:310–324.

_____. 1973. *Congressmen in Committees.* Boston: Little, Brown.

Ferejohn, John. 1974. *Pork Barrel Politics: Rivers and Harbors Legislation, 1947–1968.* Stanford: Stanford University Press.

_____. 1983. "Congress and Redistribution." In Allen Schick, ed., *Making Economic Policy in Congress.* Washington, D.C.: American Enterprise Institute.

Fiorina, Morris P. 1977. *Congress: Keystone of the Washington Establishment.* New Haven: Yale University Press.

_____. 1983. "Flagellating the Federal Bureaucracy." *Society* (20):66–74.

Fischer, Gerald. 1961. *Bank Holding Companies.* New York : Columbia University Press.

_____. 1968. *American Banking Structure.* New York: Columbia University Press.

Freeman, J. Leiper. 1955, 1965. *The Political Process.* New York: Random House.

Gais, Thomas L., Mark A. Peterson, and Jack L. Walker. 1984. "Interest Groups, Iron Triangles and Representative Institutions in American National Government." *British Journal of Political Science* (14):161–185.

Goggin, Malcolm O. 1986. "The 'Too Few Cases/Too Many Variables' Problem in Implementation Research." *Western Political Quarterly* (June):328–347.

Gormley, William T. 1983. *The Politics of Public Utility Regulation.* Pittsburgh: University of Pittsburgh Press.

_____. 1986. "Regulatory Issue Networks in a Federal System." *Polity* 18(Summer): 595–620.

Gouge, William M. 1833 (1968). *A Short History of Money and Banking in the United States.* New York: Augustus M. Kelly.

Gregg, Gail. 1979a. "House Attaches Federal Reserve Bill to Sweeping Senate Bank Measure." *Congressional Quarterly Weekly Report* (November 10):2546–2548.

_____. 1979b. "Banking Bill Impasse." *Congressional Quarterly Weekly Report* (December 8):2763.

_____. 1980a. "Congress Plans New Try on Banking Deregulation." *Congressional Quarterly Weekly Report* (January 12):76.

_____. 1980b. "Conferees to Resume Work on Omnibus Bank Bill." *Congressional Quarterly Weekly Report* (March 1):589.

_____. 1980c. "New Banking Law Will Lift Interest Rate Ceilings, Tighten Monetary Controls." *Congressional Quarterly Weekly Report* (April 12):964–965.

_____. 1981. "Legislative Reflection Time for Senate Banking Panel." *Congressional Quarterly Weekly Report* (March 21):503–504.

Griffith, Ernest S. 1939. *The Impasse of Democracy.* New York: Harrison Hilton Books.

Gross, Bertram M. 1953. *The Legislative Struggle.* New York: McGraw-Hill.

Hackley, Howard. 1966. "Our Baffling Banking System." *Virginia Law Review* 52(May): 565–632.

Hall, Richard L., and Bernard Grofman. 1990. "The Committee Assignment Process and the Conditional Nature of Committee Bias." *American Political Science Review* 84(December):1149–1166.

Hamm, Keith E. 1983. "Patterns of Influence Among Committees, Agencies and Interest Groups." *Legislative Studies Quarterly* 7(August):379–426.

_____. 1986. "The Role of 'Subgovernments' in US State Policy Making." *Legislative Studies Quarterly* 11(August):321–351.

_____. 1987. "The Prevalence of Subgovernments: Evidence from Nebraska State Legislative Committee Decision Making." Paper presented at the Midwest Political Science Meeting, Chicago, Illinois, April 9–11.

Hammond, Bray. 1957. *Banks and Politics in America from the Revolution to the Civil War.* Princeton: Princeton University Press.

Hammond, Thomas H., and Jack H. Knott. 1988. "The Deregulatory Snowball: Explaining Deregulation in the Financial Industry." *Journal of Politics* 50:3–30.

Harris, Richard A., and Sidney M. Milkis. 1989. *The Politics of Regulatory Change.* New York: Oxford University Press.

Heclo, Hugh. 1978. "Issue Networks and the Executive Establishment." In Anthony King, ed., *The New American Political System.* Washington, D.C.: AEI Press.

Heinberg, John G. 1926 (1974). *The Office of the Comptroller of the Currency.* New York: AMS Press.

Heintz, Theodore H. 1988. "Advocacy Coalitions and the OCS Leasing Debate: A Case Study in Policy Evolution." *Policy Sciences* 21:213–238.

Hjren, Ben, and David O. Porter. 1981. "Implementation Structures: A New Unit of Administrative Analysis." *Organization Studies* 2–3:211–227.

Huitt, Ralph K. 1968. "Political Feasibility." In Austin Ranney, ed., *Political Science and Public Policy*. Chicago: Markham.

_____. 1973. "The Internal Distribution of Influence: The Senate." In David Truman, ed., *The Congress and America's Future*. Englewood Cliffs: Prentice-Hall, pp. 91–117.

Ingraham, Patricia W., and David H. Rosenbloom. 1992. *The Promise and Paradox of Civil Service Reform*. Pittsburgh: University of Pittsburgh Press.

Jenkins-Smith, Hank C. 1988. "Analytical Debates and Policy Learning: Analysis and Change in the Federal Bureaucracy." *Policy Sciences* 21:169–211.

Jesse, Michael. 1977. *Bank Holding Companies and the Public Interest*. Lexington, Mass.: Lexington Books.

Johnson, Cathy Marie. 1992. *The Dynamics of Conflict Between Bureaucrats and Legislators*. New York: M. E. Sharpe.

Jones, Bryan, Frank Baumgartner, and Jeffrey Talbert. 1993. "The Destruction of Issue Monopolies in Congress." *American Political Science Review* 87(September):657–671.

Jones, Charles O. 1961. "Representation in Congress: The Case of the House Agricultural Committee." *American Political Science Review* 55:358–367.

_____. 1982. *The United States Congress: People, Place and Policy*. Homewood, Ill.: Dorsey Press.

_____. 1984. 3rd ed. *An Introduction to the Study of Public Policy*. Monterey, Calif.: Brooks/Cole.

Kaufman, George S., and Roger C. Kormendi, eds. 1986. *Deregulating Financial Services: Public Policy in Flux*. Cambridge: Ballinger.

Kelman, Steven. 1981. *Regulating America, Regulating Sweden: A Comparative Study of Occupational Safety and Health Policy*. Cambridge: MIT Press.

Kemp, Kathleen A. 1981. "Symbolic and Strict Regulation in the American States." *Social Science Quarterly* 62(September):516–526.

Kennedy, Susan E. 1973. *The Banking Crisis of 1933*. Lexington: University of Kentucky Press.

Kettl, Donald F. 1986. *Leadership at the Fed*. New Haven: Yale University Press.

Kingdon, John W. 1966. "A House Appropriations Subcommittee: Influences on the Budgetary Process." *Southwestern Social Science Quarterly* 47:69–78.

_____. 1984. *Agendas, Alternatives, and Public Policies*. Boston: Little, Brown.

Kiser, L., and E. Ostrom. 1982. "The Three Worlds of Action." In Elinor Ostrom, ed., *Strategies of Political Inquiry*. Beverly Hills: Sage.

Kozak, David C. 1984. *Contexts of Congressional Decision Behavior*. New York: University Press of America.

Krasnow, Erwin G., and Lawrence D. Longley. 1978. *The Politics of Broadcast Regulation*. New York: St. Martin's Press.

Krehbiel, Keith. 1990. "Are Congressional Committees Composed of Preference Outliers?" *American Political Science Review* 84(March):149–164.

_____. 1991. *Information and Legislative Organization*. Ann Arbor: University of Michigan Press.

Lamb, Ralph W. 1962. *Group Banking*. New Brunswick, N.J.: Rutgers University Press.

Lasswell, Harold D. 1958. *Politics: Who Gets What, When, How*. Cleveland: World.

Latham, Earl. 1952. *The Group Basis of Politics*. Ithaca, N.Y.: Cornell University Press.

Leyden, Kevin. 1995. "Interest Group Resources and Testimony at Congressional Hearings." *Legislative Studies Quarterly* (August):431–439.

Light, Paul. 1982. *The President's Agenda*. Baltimore: Johns Hopkins University Press.

_____. 1995. *Thickening Government*. Washington, D.C.: Brookings Institution.

Livingston, James. 1986. *Origins of the Federal Reserve System*. Ithaca, N.Y.: Cornell University Press.

Long, Norton. 1962. *The Polity*. Chicago: Rand McNally.

Longley, Lawrence D., and Walter J. Oleszek. 1989. *Bicameral Politics: Conference Committees in Congress*. New Haven: Yale University Press.

Lowi, Theodore J. 1969. *The End of Liberalism*. New York: W. W. Norton.

Maass, Arthur A. 1951. *Muddy Waters*. Cambridge: Harvard University Press.

MacAvoy, Paul W. 1979. *The Regulated Industries and the Economy*. New York: W. W. Norton.

Manley, John. 1965. "The House Committee on Ways and Means: Conflict Management in a Congressional Committee." *American Political Science Review* 59:927–939.

Matthews, Donald. 1960. *U.S. Senators and Their World*. New York: Random House.

Mayer, Martin. 1974. *The Bankers*. New York: Ballantine.

McCool, Daniel. 1989. "Subgovernments and the Impact of Policy Fragmentation and Accommodation." *Policy Studies Review* 8:264–287.

_____. 1990. "Subgovernments as Determinants of Political Viability." *Political Science Quarterly* 105:269–293.

McGraw, Thomas K. 1975. "Regulation in America." *Business History Review* (Summer):159–183.

_____. 1985. *Prophets of Regulation*. Cambridge: Harvard University Press.

Meier, Kenneth J. 1979. *Politics and the Bureaucracy*. North Scituate, Mass.: Duxbury Press.

_____. 1985. *Regulation*. New York: St. Martin's Press.

_____. 1988. *The Political Economy of Regulation*. Albany: State University of New York Press.

Melnick, R. Shep. 1983. *Regulation and the Courts*. Washington, D.C.: Brookings Institution.

Meyer, W. S., ed. 1934. *The State Papers and Other Writings of Herbert Hoover*. New York: Columbia University Press.

Milward, H. Brinton, and Gary L. Wamsley. 1984. "Policy Subsystems, Networks and the Tools of Public Management." In Robert Eyestone, ed., *Public Policy Formation*. Greenwood, Conn.: JAI Press.

Mints, Lloyd. 1945. *A History of Banking Theory*. Chicago: University of Chicago Press.

Mitnick, Barry. 1980. *The Political Economy of Regulation*. New York: Columbia University Press.

Moe, Terry M. 1981. "Toward a Broader View of Interest Groups." *Journal of Politics* (May):531–543.

_____. 1982. "Regulatory Performance and Presidential Administration." *American Journal of Political Science* 26(May):197–224.

Mucciaroni, Gary. 1990. *The Political Failure of Employment Policy, 1945–1982*. Pittsburgh: University of Pittsburgh Press.

Noll, Roger, and Bruce M. Owen. 1983. *The Political Economy of Deregulation*. Washington, D.C.: AEI Press.

Office of the Comptroller of the Currency. 1872. *Annual Report*. Washington, D.C.: OCC.
_____. 1873. *Annual Report*. Washington, D.C.: OCC.

Oleszek, Walter J. 1984. *Congressional Procedures and the Policy Process*. 2nd ed. Washington, D.C.: Congressional Quarterly Press.

Oppenheimer, Bruce. 1974. *Oil and the Congressional Process: The Limits of Symbolic Politics*. Lexington, Mass.: Lexington Books.

Owen, Bruce M., and Ronald Braeutigam. 1978. *The Regulation Game*. Cambridge: Ballinger.

Peltzman, Sam. 1976. "Toward a More General Theory of Regulation." *Journal of Law and Economics* 19(April):211–240.

Perkins, Lynette P. 1980. "Influences of Members' Goals on their Committee Behavior: The US House Judiciary Committee." *Legislative Studies Quarterly* 5:373–392.

Pertschuk, Michael. 1982. *Revolt Against Regulation*. Berkeley: University of California Press.

Petracca, Mark P., ed. 1992. *The Politics of Interests*. Boulder: Westview Press.

Polsby, Nelson W. 1968. "The Institutionalization of the United States House of Representatives." *American Political Science Review* 62:144–168.

Posner, Richard A. 1974. "Theories of Economic Regulation." *Bell Journal of Economics and Management Science* 5(Autumn):337–352.

Quirk, Paul J. 1981. *Industry Influence in Federal Regulatory Agencies*. Princeton: Princeton University Press.

Reagan, Michael D. 1987. *Regulation: The Politics of Policy*. Boston: Little, Brown.

Redford, Emmette S. 1962. "Preface." In James E. Anderson, *The Emergence of the Modern Regulatory State*. Washington, D.C.: Public Affairs Press.
_____. 1969. *Democracy in the Administrative State*. New York: Oxford University Press.

Redman, Eric. 1973. *The Dance of Legislation*. New York: Simon and Schuster.

Riker, William H. 1980. "Implications from the Disequilibrium of Majority Rule for the Study of Institutions." *American Political Science Review* 74:432–446.

Ripley, Randall B. 1988. *Congress: Process and Policy*. 4th ed. New York: W. W. Norton.

Ripley, Randall B., and Grace A. Franklin. 1987. 4th ed. *Congress, the Bureaucracy, and Public Policy*. Chicago: Dorsey Press.

Robertson, Ross. 1968. *The Comptroller and Bank Supervision*. Washington, D.C.: Office of the Comptroller of the Currency.

Rokeach, Milton. 1968. *Beliefs, Attitudes and Values*. San Francisco: Jossey-Bass.

Rosenman, S. I., ed. 1938. *The Public Papers and Addresses of Franklin D. Roosevelt*. vol. 1. New York: Columbia University Press.

Rourke, Francis E. 1969. *Bureaucracy, Politics and Public Policy*. Boston: Little, Brown.

Rundquist, Barry S., and John A. Ferejohn. 1975. "Observations on a Distributive Theory of Policy-Making: Two American Expenditure Programs Compared." In Craig Liske, William Loehr, and John McCamant, eds., *Comparative Public Policy: Issues, Theories, and Methods*. New York: Sage.

Rushefsky, Mark E. 1990. *Public Policy in the United States*. Pacific Grove, Calif.: Brooks/Cole.

Sabatier, Paul. 1987. "Knowledge, Policy Oriented Learning, and Policy Change." *Knowledge* 8(June):649–692.
_____. 1988. "An Advocacy Coalition Framework of Policy Change and the Role of Policy-Oriented Learning Therein." *Policy Sciences* 21:129–168.

Sabatier, Paul, and Hank Jenkins-Smith. 1993. *Policy Change and Learning: An Advocacy Coalition Approach.* Boulder: Westview Press.

Sabatier, Paul, and Niel Pelkey. 1987. "Incorporating Multiple Actors and Guidance Instruments into Models of Regulatory Policy-Making." *Administration and Society* 19(September):236–263.

Scher, Seymour. 1960. "Congressional Committee Members as Independent Agency Overseers: A Case Study." *American Political Science Review* 54:911–920.

Scholzman, Kay Lehman, and John T. Tierny. 1986. *Organized Interests and American Democracy.* New York: Harper and Row.

Schroedel, Jean Roth. 1994. *Congress, the President, and Policymaking.* Armonk, N.Y.: M. E. Sharpe.

Shepsle, Kenneth A. 1978. *The Giant Jigsaw Puzzle.* Chicago: University of Chicago Press.

Smith, Steve, and Christopher Deering. 1990. *Committees in Congress, 2nd ed.* Washington, D.C.: Congressional Quarterly Press.

Stewart, Joseph J. 1991. "Policy Models and Equal Educational Opportunity." *PS: Political Science and Politics* 24(June):167–173.

Stigler, George. 1971. "The Theory of Economic Regulation." *Bell Journal of Economics and Management Science.* 2(Spring):3–21.

Stone, Alan. 1977. *Economic Regulation and the Public Interest.* Ithaca, N.Y.: Cornell University Press.

_____. 1982. *Regulation and Its Alternatives.* Washington, D.C.: CQ Press.

Talbert, Jeffrey C., Bryan D. Jones, and Frank R. Baumgartner. 1995. "Nonlegislative Hearings and Policy Change in Congress." *American Journal of Political Science* (May):383–405.

Tate, Dale, 1981. "House Votes Emergency Aid for Ailing S&Ls; Senate Weighs Broader Bill." *Congressional Quarterly Weekly Report* (October 31):2106–2107.

_____. 1982. "Limited Banking Reform Bill Awaits Floor Activity in Senate." *Congressional Quarterly Weekly Report* (August 28):2125–2126.

Taus, Ester Rogoff. 1943. *Central Banking Functions of the United States Treasury 1789–1941.* New York: Columbia University Press.

Taylor, Jeremy F. 1989. *The Banking System in Troubled Times: New Issues of Stability and Continuity.* New York: Quorum Books.

_____. 1990. *The Process of Change in American Banking.* New York: Quorum Books.

Thurber, James A. 1991. "Dynamics of Policy Subsystems in American Politics." In Allan J. Cigler and Burdett A. Loomis, eds., *Interest Group Politics.* 3rd ed. Washington, D.C.: CQ Press.

Trescott, Paul B. 1963. *Financing American Enterprise.* New York: Harper and Row.

Truman, David. 1951. *The Governmental Process.* New York: Knopf.

U.S. Congress, House. 1963. Hearings before the Committee on Banking and Currency. *Increased Flexibility for Financial Institutions.* 88th Cong., 1st sess., H.R. 5845, 7878, 8230, 8245, 8247, 8459, and 8541.

_____. 1965. Hearings before the Committee on Banking and Currency. *To Permit National Banks to Underwrite and Deal in "Revenue Bonds."* 89th Cong., 1st sess., H.R. 7539.

_____. 1971. Hearings before the Committee on Banking and Currency. *The Banking Reform Act of 1971.* 92nd Cong., 1st sess., H.R. 5700, 3287, and 7440.

_____. 1973a. Hearings before the Subcommittee on Bank Supervision and Insurance of the Committee on Banking and Currency. *Regulation Q, NOW Accounts, Investment in State Housing Corporations.* 93rd Cong., 1st sess., H.R. 4070, 4719, and 4988.

_____. 1973b. Hearings before the Subcommittee on Bank Supervision and Insurance of the Committee on Banking and Currency. *The Credit Crunch and Reform of Financial Institutions.* 93rd Cong., 1st sess.

_____. 1975a. Hearings before the Subcommittee on Financial Institutions Supervision, Regulation and Insurance of the Committee on Banking, Currency and Housing. *Bank Failures.* 94th Cong., 1st sess.

_____. 1975b. Hearings before the Subcommittee on Financial Institutions Supervision, Regulation and Insurance of the Committee on Banking, Currency and Housing. *Financial Institutions and the Nation's Economy (FINE) "Discussion Principles."* 94th Cong., 1st and 2nd sess.

_____. 1979a. Hearings before the Subcommittee on Financial Institutions Supervision, Regulation and Insurance of the Committee on Banking, Currency and Housing. *Monetary Control.* 96th Cong., 1st sess.

_____. 1979b. Hearings before the Subcommittee on Financial Institutions Supervision, Regulation and Insurance of the Committee on Banking, Currency and Housing. *Amending the Financial Institutions Regulatory and Interest Rate Control Act.* 96th Cong., 1st sess.

_____. 1980a. Hearings before the Subcommittee on Financial Institutions Supervision, Regulation and Insurance of the Committee on Banking, Currency and Housing. *Oversight Hearings on the Depository Institutions Deregulation Committee.* 96th Cong., 2nd sess.

_____. 1980b. Hearings before the Subcommittee on Financial Institutions Supervision, Regulation and Insurance of the Committee on Banking, Currency and Housing. *Regulation Q.* 96th Cong., 2nd sess.

_____. 1981a. Hearings before the Subcommittee on Financial Institutions Supervision, Regulation and Insurance of the Committee on Banking, Currency and Housing. *Oversight Hearings on the Depository Institutions Deregulation Committee.* 97th Cong., 1st sess.

_____. 1981b. Hearings before the Subcommittee on Financial Institutions Supervision, Regulation and Insurance of the Committee on Banking, Currency and Housing. *Financial Institutions in a Revolutionary Era.* 97th Cong., 1st sess.

_____. 1981c. Hearings before the Subcommittee on Financial Institutions Supervision, Regulation and Insurance of the Committee on Banking, Currency and Housing. *Depository Institutions Amendments of 1982.* 97th Cong., 2nd sess.

U.S. Congress, Senate. 1947. Hearings before the Committee on Banking and Currency. 80th Cong., 1st sess., S. 829.

_____. 1950. Hearings before the Committee on Banking and Currency, Subcommittee on the Federal Reserve. 81st Cong., 2nd sess., S. 2318.

_____. 1953. Hearings before the Committee on Banking and Currency. 83rd Cong., 1st sess., S. 76 and 1118.

_____. 1955. Hearings before the Committee on Banking and Currency. *Control of Bank Holding Companies.* 84th Cong., 1st sess., S. 880, 2350, and H.R. 6227.

_____. 1956. Hearings before the Committee on Banking and Currency. *Control of Bank Holding Companies.* 84th Cong., 2nd sess., S. 2577.

_____. 1973a. Hearings before the Subcommittee on Financial Institutions of the Committee on Banking, Housing, and Urban Affairs. *Financial Structure and Regulation.* 93rd Cong., 1st sess.

_____. 1973b. Hearings before the Subcommittee on Financial Institutions of the Committee on Banking, Housing, and Urban Affairs. *Financial Institutions Act.* 93rd Cong., 2nd sess., S. 2591.

_____. 1975. Hearings before the Subcommittee on Financial Institutions of the Committee on Banking, Housing, and Urban Affairs. *Financial Institutions Act of 1975.* 94th Cong., 1st sess., S. 1267, 1475, and 1540.

_____. 1977a. Hearings before the Subcommittee on Financial Institutions of the Committee on Banking, Housing, and Urban Affairs. *First Meeting on the Condition of the Banking System.* 95th Cong., 1st sess.

_____. 1977b. Hearings before the Subcommittee on Financial Institutions of the Committee on Banking, Housing, and Urban Affairs. *Competition in Banking Act.* 95th Cong., 1st sess.

_____. 1979a. Hearings before the Subcommittee on Financial Institutions of the Committee on Banking, Housing, and Urban Affairs. *Depository Institutions Deregulation Act of 1979.* 96th Cong., 1st sess.

_____. 1979b. Hearings before the Subcommittee on Financial Institutions of the Committee on Banking, Housing, and Urban Affairs. *Third Meeting on the Condition of the Banking System.* 96th Cong., 1st sess.

_____. 1980a. Hearings before the Subcommittee on Financial Institutions of the Committee on Banking, Housing, and Urban Affairs. *Competition in Banking Act of 1980.* 96th Cong., 2nd sess.

_____. 1980b. Hearings before the Subcommittee on Financial Institutions of the Committee on Banking, Housing, and Urban Affairs. *Depository Institutions Deregulation Committee.* 96th Cong., 2nd sess.

_____. 1980c. Hearings before the Subcommittee on Financial Institutions of the Committee on Banking, Housing, and Urban Affairs. *Fourth Meeting on the Condition of the Banking System.* 96th Cong., 2nd sess.

_____. 1981a. Hearings before the Subcommittee on Financial Institutions of the Committee on Banking, Housing, and Urban Affairs. *Financial Institutions Restructuring and Services Act of 1981.* 97th Cong., 1st sess.

_____. 1981b. Hearings before the Subcommittee on Financial Institutions of the Committee on Banking, Housing, and Urban Affairs. *Competition and Conditions in the Financial System.* 97th Cong., 1st sess.

Walker, Jack. 1977. "Setting the Agenda in the United States Senate." *British Journal of Politics* 7(October):423–445.

_____. 1983. "The Origins and Maintenance of Interest Groups in America." *American Political Science Review* 77:390–406.

Weingest, Barry, and Mark Moran. 1983. "Bureaucratic Discretion or Congressional Control?" *Journal of Political Economy* 91:765–800.

Weiss, Carol H. 1977. "Research for Policy's Sake: The Enlightenment Function of Social Research." *Policy Analysis* 3(Fall):531–545.

_____. 1983. "Ideology, Interest, and Information." In Daniel Callahan and Bruce Jennings, eds., *Ethics, the Social Sciences, and Policy Analysis.* New York: Plenum Press.

West, Robert. 1977. *Banking Reform and the Federal Reserve.* Ithaca, N.Y.: Cornell University Press.

White, Eugene. 1983. *The Regulation and Reform of the American Banking System.* Princeton: Princeton University Press.

White, George C. 1980. "Payment Systems Today—and Tomorrow." *Bankers Magazine* 163(March-April):26–31.

Wiebe, Robert H. 1963. *Businessmen and Reform: A Study of the Progressive Movement.* Cambridge: Harvard University Press.

Wilburn, Jean A. 1967. *Biddle's Bank: The Crucial Years.* New York: Columbia University Press.

Wilson, Graham K. 1981. *Interest Groups in the United States.* New York: Oxford University Press.

Wilson, James Q. 1980. *The Politics of Regulation.* New York: Basic Books.

Wilson, James Q., and Patricia Rachal. 1977. "Can Government Regulate Itself?" *Public Interest* (Winter):3–14.

Wilson, Woodrow. 1885 (1973). *Congressional Government: A Study in American Politics.* Gloucester, Maine: Peter Smith.

Zeigler, Harmon. 1964. *Interest Groups in American Society.* Englewood Cliffs, N.J.: Prentice-Hall.

About the Book and Author

Questions of influence are at the heart of political science. A particularly compelling answer to the question of who wields influence takes the form of subsystems theory. Combining detailed historiographical and quantitative analysis, Jeffrey Worsham tracks, explains, and explores the policy consequences of political variation in the financial subsystem from its inception through the 1990s, arguing that subsystems are a wavering-equilibrium solution to the problem of policymaking in the United States.

The book answers three interrelated questions with regard to the wavering-equilibrium solution. First, what have been the major patterns of participation, or political variation, in the financial subsystem for the first 100 years of its existence? Second, what accounts for those patterns and the change from one type of politics to another? Finally, what are the consequences of different types of subsystem politics for public policy?

Jeffrey Worsham is assistant professor of political science at West Virginia University.

Index

DIDMCA. *See* Depository Institutions
  Deregulatory and Monetary Control
  Act of 1980
Dingell, John, 124–128
Discounting, 35, 142(n9)
Distributive policy, 3–4, 75–76, 80, 134
  and outsiders, 78, 82
Dominant coalitions, 3–5, 7, 129. *See also*
  Iron triangle
  and belief systems, 14
  and bill introduction, 68–73, 78
  and distributive policy, 80–81
  and hearings, 50–51, 66
  as monopoly, 4

Eccles, Marriner, 43–44, 46, 93, 95, 105,
  144(n2)
Economic dislocation, 11–12, 90, 94, 111,
  118, 122, 131–132
Economists, 110–112
EFTs. *See* Electronic fund transfers
Eisenhower, Dwight D., 99
Electronic fund transfers (EFTs), 117
Elites, 1, 2
Emergency Banking Act, 39
Entrepreneur, role of, 28–29
Equilibrium, 17, 56, 68, 104, 116, 137–138
Experts, 11, 31, 133

FDIC. *See* Federal Deposit Insurance
  Corporation
Fed. *See* Federal Reserve
Federal Advisory Council, 95
Federal Deposit Insurance Corporation
  (FDIC), 21–22, 102, 110, 112–114,
  121, 126, 128, 133
Federal Home Loan Bank Board (FHLBB),
  23, 110, 116, 121–123, 128, 133
Federal Home Loan Mortgage
  Corporation, 23
Federal Reserve, 22
  and chambers of Congress, 55
  and deregulation, 112, 114–115, 128
  and holding companies, 90–92
  hybrid regulation of, 32–33
  and outsiders, 64
  and policy core beliefs, 25, 32

and private banks, 25–26
and programs, 25
Federal Reserve Act, 18, 22, 24–25, 31–34,
  41, 46, 142(n5)
Federal Reserve Board, 32, 43–44, 102, 133
Federal Savings and Loan Insurance
  Corporation (FSLIC), 23, 124, 126,
  133
Feedback, 15–16, 90, 94, 97, 100, 101, 111,
  113, 118, 122, 125
Fenno, Richard, 10
FHLBB. *See* Federal Home Loan Bank
  Board
*Financial Institutions and the Nations
  Economy (FINE)*, 109, 112–117
*FINE. See Financial Institutions and the
  Nations Economy*
First Bankcorp, 89
Fletcher, Duncan, 40
Fowler, Charles N., 28–29, 37, 46, 133
FSLIC. *See* Federal Savings and Loan
  Insurance Corporation

Gage, Lyman, 28
Garn, Jake, 121–123, 133, 134
Garner, John Nance, 41
Garn-St. Germain bill, 109, 120–123
Glass, Carter, 31–33, 36–38, 40–41, 92
  and Banking Act of 1935, 43–44
Glass-McAdoo bill, 90–92, 95
Gore, Thomas P., 40
Gormley, William, 11
Great Depression, 13, 34, 55, 92, 131. *See
  also* New Deal

Hamm, Keith, 8, 49, 143(n1)
Hearings
  and agenda, 64
  participation profiles, 50–51, 58–61, 68,
    110–112
  and salience, 66
Heclo, Hugh, 3, 5
Holding companies, 19
  history of, 88–89
  and one-bank loophole, 102, 103
  and policy core beliefs, 90–91, 96–97,
    100–101